# ENGLISH IN GLOBAL CONTEXTS:

# ANSWER KEY

Proficiency Tasks
for
Aspiring Learners

JJ POLK

GLOBAL TOUCHSTONES

English in Global Contexts: Answer Key
Proficiency Tasks for Aspiring Learners

Copyright © 2015 JJ Polk

All Rights Reserved. No part of this book may be reproduced in any form or by any means, electronic or mechanical, including photocopying, recording, or by any information storage and retrieval system, without permission in writing from the author and publisher.

ISBN: 978-0-9909086-1-6

Published by:
Global Touchstones
Los Angeles, CA

Cover and interior design by Stacey Aaronson

Printed in the United States of America

# CONTENTS

| | | |
|---|---|---|
| UNIT 1 | HE SAYS ... SHE SAYS | 1 |
| UNIT 2 | IT TAKES ALL KINDS OF PEOPLE | 8 |
| UNIT 3 | DIFFERENT STROKES FOR DIFFERENT FOLKS | 15 |
| UNIT 4 | ENGLISH AS THE GLOBAL LINGUA FRANCA | 22 |
| UNIT 5 | SOCIAL NETWORKS AND THE REVOLUTION IN COMMUNICATION | 29 |
| UNIT 6 | MONEY MAKES THE WORLD GO ROUND | 36 |
| UNIT 7 | STOCKS, BONDS, AND WHAT WENT WRONG | 42 |
| UNIT 8 | ALPHA CITIES AND MEGACITIES | 49 |
| UNIT 9 | ENGINEERING MARVELS | 55 |
| UNIT 10 | GOING TO EXTREMES | 62 |
| UNIT 11 | NATURE'S AWESOME POWER AND LINGERING SECRETS | 68 |
| UNIT 12 | OUR BRAVE NEW WORLD | 75 |

# HE SAYS ... SHE SAYS

## UNIT 1

CLOZE TASK / READING PASSAGE: Suggested answers [responses may vary].

**CLOZE TASK ANSWERS**

[1] distinguish (also possible, but less likely: differentiate)
[2] apart
[3] front
[4] out
[5] guess
[6] to
[7] himself
[8] that
[9] enters
[10] taken / removed
[11] wonder
[12] each
[13] Never
[14] less
[15] when
[16] tried
[17] mirror
[18] say
[19] far
[20] happens / chances
[21] event
[22] after
[23] hate / detest / dislike / loathe
[24] roles
[25] explain
[26] clothes
[27] conversation
[28] watch / rear / raise / guard
[29] taking
[30] number
[31] being / getting
[32] sexes / genders
[33] Far
[34] This
[35] provide / equip

# VOCABULARY WORK ANSWERS

## PART A

| From Paragraphs A–G: | Synonymous Word or Phrase |
|---|---|
| 1. fondled; touched gently | CARESSED (D) |
| 2. continually; perpetually; recurringly | PERENNIALLY (B) |
| 3. most modest; most unpretentious | HUMBLEST (F) |
| 4. the art and skill of a magician or warlock | WIZARDRY (G) |
| 5. incredible; unbelievable; astounding; strange; weird | UNCANNY (B) |
| 6. pertaining to colors | CHROMATIC (E) |
| 7. ascribed to; assigned to; credited with | ATTRIBUTED (A) |
| 8. unnecessary; unneeded; not required | SUPERFLUOUS (G) |
| 9. outing; fling; adventure; romp | SPREE (C) |
| 10. overt; obvious | BLATANT (A) |
| 11. on pins and needles; restless; antsy; apprehensive | ANXIOUS (F) |
| 12. lacking; deprived of; wanting; without | DEVOID OF (G) |
| 13. everywhere | UBIQUITOUS (A) |
| 14. grain; structure; fabric; surface | TEXTURE (F) |
| 15. cots (especially for medical use); pallets | STRETCHERS (C) |
| 16. verbal nonsense; jabber | GIBBERISH (G) |
| 17. wandering; unfocused; uneven; erratic | RAMBLING (G) |
| 18. aired (verb); televised | BROADCAST (A) |
| 19. enticing; alluring | TEMPTING (E) |
| 20. nothing; nil | NOUGHT (F) |
| 21. related to the structure of the body | ANATOMICAL (A) |
| 22. unvarying; unchanging; dull; boring | MONOTONOUS (G) |
| 23. adventures; pleasure trips; excursions | OUTINGS (C & G) |
| 24. repeated; reproduced; reduplicated | REPLICATED (E) |

# UNIT ONE | HE SAYS ... SHE SAYS

| From Paragraphs H–N: | Synonymous Word or Phrase |
|---|---|
| 25. deeds; achievements | FEATS (J) |
| 26. outline; contour; profile; shape | SILHOUETTE (I) |
| 27. emphasizing; pointing out; stressing | HIGHLIGHTING (K) |
| 28. chase; hunt; quest | PURSUIT (J) |
| 29. to transition uninterruptedly from one point or element to another | SEGUE (I) |
| 30. effectively; pertinently; forcefully; persuasively; authoritatively; convincingly | COGENTLY (K) |
| 31. scents; aromas | FRAGRANCES (I) |
| 32. elements; parts | COMPONENTS (L) |
| 33. pliability; malleability; flexibility; adaptability | PLASTICITY (L) |
| 34. riddle; mystery; enigma | PUZZLE (J) |
| 35. empathy; mercy; sympathy; pity; kind-heartedness | COMPASSION (J) |
| 36. to quote; to refer to | CITE (J) |

## PART B

VOCABULARY WORK ANSWERS

1. In many cities, significant increases in air pollution have rightly been ATTRIBUTED to a substantial rise in the numbers of private cars.

2. Most of our editing work on the manuscript involved eliminating redundancies and other SUPERFLUOUS verbiage.

3. In the Constitution of the United States of America, "life, liberty, and the PURSUIT of happiness" are declared to be inalienable rights granted to all human beings.

4. The results of studies purportedly showing neutrinos traveling faster than the speed of light could not be REPLICATED, thus casting doubt on the methods of measurement used in the experiments.

5. Declining reading, math, and science test scores in many western countries have HIGHLIGHTED the need for fresh approaches to teaching and curriculum design.

6. Throughout much of the industrial era, major manufacturers showed a BLATANT disregard for the environment by dumping thousands of tons of toxic waste into rivers, streams, and oceans.

7. With its 787 carbon fiber composite aircraft, Boeing embarked on a questionable approach to manufacturing the jet, as essentially all of its COMPONENT parts are constructed separately in many different countries and are then flown back to the U.S. for final assembly.

8. When PURSUING dangerous criminals, Interpol makes extensive use of continent-wide databases containing millions of images that are quickly processed using highly accurate face recognition software.

9. In regions of the world that do not experience four distinct seasons, periodic changes often SEGUE so smoothly and subtly from one into the other that many observers might find it difficult to describe what changes were even noticeable.

10. Neutrinos are among nature's most UBIQUITOUS particles, with as many as 65 billion per second passing through every square centimeter of any region on earth perpendicular to the sun, including our own bodies.

11. Most of the students in the lecture were put to sleep by the speaker's unwavering, MONOTONOUS voice.

12. One of the worst things any candidate for a job opening can do during an interview is to RAMBLE aimlessly from topic to topic without any clear focus.

13. Every four years, most people around the world are able to view live BROADCASTS of the opening ceremonies of the Olympics.

14. Johann Sebastian Bach's extemporaneous composition and performance of a four-part fugue was described by MIT artificial intelligence expert Douglas Hofstatter as a super-human FEAT, equivalent to playing 64 games of chess blindfolded and winning all of them.

UNIT ONE | HE SAYS ... SHE SAYS

15. In the wake of the 2008 global financial crisis, international teams of legal and economic experts <u>COGENTLY</u> argued the case for an international regulatory body to supervise complex markets such as those involving derivatives.

16. Many high-tech industries rely on rare earth elements for a number of <u>COMPONENTS</u> in their most advanced products.

## PART C

LANGUAGE FOCUS ANSWERS

1. In paragraphs A–H, identify 10 unreduced relative clauses and specify the noun or pronoun that they modify. [For a review of the grammar of RELATIVE CLAUSES, see the APPENDIX, section B.]

   i)    *that distinguish men from women* modifies *differences*
   ii)   *that set men and women apart* modifies *features*
   iii)  *that might attempt to compete* modifies *natural occurrences*
   iv)   *who happens to find himself on a shopping outing* modifies *husband*
   v)    *that science has to offer* modifies *all*
   vi)   *that stand ready at the waiting* modifies *stretchers*
   vii)  *that looks promising* modifies *rack*
   viii) *that strikes fear into the heart* modifies *ritual*
   ix)   *that that was only the first store!* modifies *realization*
   x)    *who shares his zeal for the same model* modifies *someone*

2. In paragraphs A–H, identify four reduced relative clauses and specify the noun or pronoun that they modify.

   i)   *attributed to the mind itself* modifies *features*
   ii)  *heard from many women around the world* modifies *complaint*
   iii) *perennially ranked near the top* modifies *habit*
   iv)  *spent in communion locked* modifies *hours*

3. Identify one reduced relative clause that has been placed at the beginning of the sentence, pre-positional to the noun subject it modifies.

   *Singularly transfixed on the play-by-play development of the game, ...*

4. Identify words or phrases of middle to low register that indicate familiarity or emotional closeness. [For a review of REGISTER in English, see the APPENDIX, section A.]

   *honey; yeah; man; maxed out; until she drops*

5. What does the pronoun "others" refer to in the phrase in paragraph F: "There are 47 others …"?

   *stores*

## Sentence Transformation

6. No one knows the number of people who suffer from some form of addiction.
   
   **guess**
   
   It's <u>anyone's guess how many</u> people suffer from some form of addiction.

7. Carlos can't even balance his own checkbook, let alone someone else's.
   
   **mention**
   
   Carlos can't even balance his own checkbook, <u>not to mention</u> someone else's.

8. It's often difficult to distinguish identical twins if you look solely at physical features.
   
   **tell**
   
   It's often difficult <u>to tell identical twins apart</u> if you look solely at physical features.

9. Your son is quite lazy, but he can still pass the course if he tries his best.
   
   **say**
   
   Your son is quite lazy, but that is <u>not to say he can't pass</u> the course if he tries his best.

10. The mediation board will resolve any disputes that might arise in the future.
    
    **ironed**
    
    Future disputes will <u>be ironed out by</u> the mediation board.

UNIT ONE | HE SAYS ... SHE SAYS

## PART D

### Sentence Reconstruction

ULTIMATE CHALLENGE ANSWERS

1. Gender-specific behavior patterns most likely result from the combined effects of nature and nurture. {Also possible}: Most gender-specific behavior patterns likely result from the combined effects of nature and nurture.

2. Evolutionary biologists argue that the superior female ability to multitask derives from her care-giving role in early human societies.

3. During sporting events, enthusiastic male fans often appear oblivious to the world around them.

4. The findings of studies attempting to prove clear distinctions between the male and female brain are inconclusive.

5. Women seem to pay more attention to colors than men do.

6. Male game enthusiasts do not always want to verbalize their thoughts.

7. Advertisers routinely rely on stereotypical gender roles to market their products.

8. Recent studies have shown that the brain is plastic and dynamic rather than static and immutable as previously believed.

9. Studies that emphasize gender differences enjoy a greater likelihood of getting published than do those that focus on the similarities between genders.

10. Studies investigating the effects of early musical training on cognitive development confirm that the brain actively adapts to input from the environment.

# UNIT 2 — IT TAKES ALL KINDS OF PEOPLE

## CLOZE TASK ANSWERS

CLOZE TASK / READING PASSAGE: Suggested answers [responses may vary].

[1] psychiatrist / psychologist
[2] critique / criticism
[3] designation
[4] determining
[5] descriptive
[6] weaknesses
[7] directedness / direction
[8] directed
[9] joy / enjoyment
[10] acquaintances
[11] speculation
[12] pondering
[13] gathering
[14] energized
[15] obligatory
[16] recruitment / recruiting
[17] combination

[18] applicants
[19] boundaries
[20] inclinations
[21] dominant
[22] choice
[23] allowing
[24] judgment
[25] vibrant
[26] marketing
[27] charismatic
[28] reflective
[29] embodied
[30] appreciation
[31] creative
[32] preconceived
[33] numerous
[34] convincingly

# UNIT TWO | IT TAKES ALL KINDS OF PEOPLE

[35] furthered
[36] collaboration
[37] negotiators
[38] reportedly
[39] reliable
[40] culturally
[41] finance / financial
[42] management / managers
[43] marriage
[44] harmonize
[45] awake
[46] malicious
[47] expertise
[48] specialists
[49] consistently
[50] irreconcilable

## PART A

From Paragraphs A–G:  Synonymous Word or Phrase

1. look for; try to find — SEEK OUT (C)
2. transmitted (as for example information) — CONVEYED (F)
3. clamorous; rocking; noisy; rowdy — BOISTEROUS (G)
4. aimed at; pointed at; brought against — LEVELED AGAINST (B)
5. famous; well known — RENOWNED (B)
6. satisfied; pleased; at ease — CONTENT (F)
7. played down; understated; toned down; subdued — LOW-KEY (G)
8. series; suite; set — BATTERY (B)
9. changing; flowing; shifting — FLUID (E)
10. results; consequences — OUTCOMES (C)
11. recovering; getting better; on the mend — RECUPERATING (C)
12. extract; obtain; secure; get; procure — DERIVE (C)
13. quiet; hushed; tranquil; peaceful — SUBDUED (G)
14. ensuing; following; succeeding; next — SUBSEQUENT (B)
15. emphasize; underscore; highlight; stress — POINT OUT (E)
16. win over; talk into; influence; convince; bring around — SWAY (F)

> VOCABULARY WORK ANSWERS

| | |
|---|---|
| 17. equivocal; ambivalent; indefinite; vague | AMBIGUOUS (F) |
| 18. previously cited or referenced | AFOREMENTIONED (G) |

| From Paragraphs H–O: | Synonymous Word or Phrase |
|---|---|
| 19. evoke; elicit; extract | BRING OUT (I) |
| 20. hesitant; disinclined; averse to; unwilling | RELUCTANT (H) |
| 21. attendant; accompanying | CONCOMITANT (H) |
| 22. comprehend; understand; probe the depths of | FATHOM (K) |
| 23. urbane; gracious; elegant; refined | DEBONAIR (J) |
| 24. reserved; reticent; frosty; standoffish | ALOOF (K) |
| 25. notoriety; eminence; fame; prominence | LIMELIGHT (J) |
| 26. dissonance; disharmony; conflict | DISCORD (N) |
| 27. to be adapted to; to harmonize with | TO FIT IN (M) |
| 28. exhilarated; ebullient; vivacious; profuse | EXUBERANT (M) |
| 29. estrange; shut out; exclude | ALIENATE (I) |
| 30. launch; propel | CATAPULT (J) |
| 31. chose; selected | OPTED FOR (O) |
| 32. mentally deranged; insane | PSYCHOTIC (M) |
| 33. mortal enemies; foes | NEMESES (L) |
| 34. wading through; sifting through; screening; sorting through | COMBING (O) |
| 35. a boisterous dance party | RAVE (O) |
| 36. practical; utilitarian; businesslike | PRAGMATIC (J) |
| 37. being in debt; operating at a loss | IN THE RED (I) |
| 38. boring; unexciting; tiresome | DULL (J) |

## PART B

1. Precisely why so many of us DERIVE such great pleasure from wonderful music remains a true enigma.

2. The board of directors essentially cast all previous arguments aside and adopted a very PRAGMATIC approach by conducting a cost / benefit analysis.

3. We were provided with a wide array of high-tech equipment to choose from in completing the commissioned landscape photographic series, but in the end we OPTED FOR a traditional 4x5-inch film camera because of the superior image quality and flexibility.

4. Both husband and wife expressed quite DISCORDANT views on their respective roles in caring for the children, and this naturally led to frequent heated arguments.

5. Studies have shown that immigrants who were extremely successful in their home countries often experience the greatest emotional problems in trying to FIT IN WITH and adapt to the new host society.

6. SUBSEQUENT to our last meeting, a number of new developments have made our previous decisions rather untenable.

7. The mellifluous FLUIDITY of his speech was matched only by his astounding range of vocabulary and his perfect pronunciation.

8. Standard practice in most business and professional environments is the written CONVEYANCE of congratulatory remarks when an employee is promoted into a higher position.

9. The court will inform us of the OUTCOME of the trial as soon as the jury has completed its deliberations.

10. For many people, the boundaries between justified suspicion and outright jealousy are quite FLUID.

11. Even Albert Einstein found certain conclusions that resulted from the equations of quantum physics difficult to FATHOM, leading him to quip that God did not play dice.

> VOCABULARY WORK ANSWERS

12. People who have spent most of their lives in one type of culture often feel a deep sense of ALIENATION when forced by circumstances to immigrate into a completely different type of culture and language environment.

13. Standardized language proficiency tests normally consist of an extensive BATTERY of components designed to measure an individual's communicative competence in several key skill areas.

14. CONCOMITANT with the increased use of English in all types of global business, academic, and research environments has been a growing demand for competent one-on-one, highly individualized instruction.

15. Concert halls with expertly designed acoustical properties usually BRING OUT the best in all musicians.

16. Emotionally disturbed children often experience great difficulty in CONVEYING their thoughts, opinions, and feelings to others.

## LANGUAGE FOCUS ANSWERS

### PART C

1. Identify the noun clauses found in paragraph F. [For a review of NOUN CLAUSES, see the APPENDIX, section B.]

    i) *Whether we fall into the category of "sensing" or "intuiting"*
    ii) *whether we choose to trust the information*
    iii) *whether we instead rely on our "gut feelings,"*
    iv) *what the correct choice of action or the right response to a given problem is.*

2. In paragraph M, identify gerunds used as subjects of sentences or clauses. [For a review of GERUNDS and INFINITIVES, see the APPENDIX, section C.]

    *singing and dancing in public*

3. In paragraphs B–F, identify fixed collocations of verbs / adjectives + prepositions. [For a review of COLLOCATIONS, see the APPENDIX, section D.]

    *according to; based on; leveled against; rely on; identified by; interested in;*

UNIT TWO | IT TAKES ALL KINDS OF PEOPLE

*external to; centered on; engaged in; exhausted from; looking for; recuperating from; required for; win out over; revealed in; depends on; conveyed to; passing judgment on*

4. Identify the infinitives of purpose in paragraph H.

    *to fulfill; to employ; to promote*

5. What word(s) could we use to replace the word "it" at the beginning of paragraph M?

    The sentence would have to be rewritten completely if we eliminated or replaced the "dummy-it" subject. An example would be: *We should note that "norms," even in their … / "Norms," even in their most individual forms of expression, are notably very strongly influenced …*

**Sentence Transformation**

6. My instincts tell me we're going the wrong way.
    **gut**
    I have <u>a gut feeling</u> we're going the wrong way.

7. Janet studied both the piano and the flute, but she was more accomplished on the flute.
    **home**
    Janet studied both the piano and the flute, but she <u>felt / was more at home</u> with the flute.

8. Even at a very early age, Midori displayed extraordinary musical talent.
    **knack**
    Even at a very early age, Midori had <u>an extraordinary knack for</u> music.

9. This project is going to be exceptionally difficult and will require your total commitment.
    **cut**
    You're certainly going to have your <u>work cut out for you</u> with this project.

10. We need to avoid any further intradepartmental strife.
    **steer**
    We need <u>to steer clear of</u> any further intradepartmental strife.

PART D

# ULTIMATE CHALLENGE ANSWERS

## Sentence Reconstruction

1. Many companies use personality tests such as the MBTI to identify the strengths and weaknesses of their employees.

2. Jung constructed his theory of psychological types around a framework of four pairs of fundamental traits.

3. Extroverts tend to favor the lively atmosphere of social gatherings over more subdued environments that lack stimulation.

4. Headhunters often employ personality profiles to find the most suitable candidate for a given position.

5. The sensing type of personality relies largely on information obtained through the five senses.

6. Relying on what seems to be an inner instinct, the intuiting personality often reaches conclusions before all the pertinent evidence has been presented.

7. In contrast to their counterparts, extroverts appear to be better adapted to a fast-paced marketing environment that requires an aggressive sales pitch.

8. Online dating services use personality profiles to match members with partners deemed to be best fits.

9. Companies and organizations often use personality tests to determine which employees are best suited for specific types of assignments.

10. Specific behavior patterns are often more readily accepted in some cultures than in others.

# DIFFERENT STROKES FOR DIFFERENT FOLKS

UNIT 3

CLOZE TASK / READING PASSAGE: Suggested answers [responses may vary].

CLOZE TASK ANSWERS

[1] both
[2] with
[3] exist
[4] place / impose
[5] the
[6] skills
[7] distinction / difference
[8] at
[9] even
[10] whose
[11] rooted
[12] up
[13] apparent / clear
[14] contrast
[15] point
[16] all
[17] differences
[18] when / after
[19] engaged / involved
[20] ran / bumped
[21] such
[22] may / often
[23] studies
[24] value
[25] that / the
[26] part
[27] to
[28] result
[29] body
[30] adopted / used / employed
[31] study
[32] these / such
[33] comparing / studying / analyzing / investigating
[34] the
[35] while / whereas

[36] how
[37] failure
[38] expand / extend / widen / broaden
[39] played
[40] which

## VOCABULARY WORK ANSWERS

### PART A

| From Paragraphs A–G: | Synonymous Word or Phrase |
|---|---|
| 1. germane to; relevant to; appertaining to | PERTAINING TO (B) |
| 2. pretense; mask; front | FAÇADE (D) |
| 3. authorized; permitted; legalized | SANCTIONED (E) |
| 4. duty; responsibility | OBLIGATION (E) |
| 5. common; everyday; routine; normal | MUNDANE (C) |
| 6. displace; supplant; override; overrule | SUPERSEDE (E) |
| 7. conveying respect and esteem; forms used to show respect | HONORIFIC (C) |
| 8. associated with; corresponding with; connected with | CORRELATED (B) |
| 9. without purpose or intention; accidentally; inadvertently | UNWITTINGLY (C) |
| 10. exile; expulsion; banishment; ouster | OSTRACISM (D) |
| 11. harmless; inoffensive | INNOCUOUS (C) |
| 12. formalized; summarized in legal code | CODIFIED (E) |
| 13. speakers in conversation | INTERLOCUTORS (B) |
| 14. evasiveness; obliqueness; implicitness | INDIRECTNESS (G) |
| 15. personal effects; personal property | BELONGINGS (E) |
| 16. angry stares; scowls | GLARES (E) |
| 17. at first | INITIALLY (G) |
| 18. develop over time | EVOLVE (B) |
| 19. unspoken; undeclared; unstated | TACIT (D) |

| | |
|---|---|
| 20. frank; candid; outspoken | BLUNT (F) |
| 21. aggressive; belligerent; antagonistic | HOSTILE (F) |
| 22. provision in law or written document; section of legal document | CLAUSE (D) |
| 23. to cover; to shroud; to veil; to disguise; to conceal | CLOAK (G) |
| 24. gauged; considered; contemplated; deliberated | WEIGHED (F) |

| From Paragraphs H–N: | Synonymous Word or Phrase |
|---|---|
| 25. praise; ovation; celebration | ACCLAIM (I) |
| 26. graces; little pleasures; trivialities | NICETIES (H) |
| 27. controversies; strife; conflicts; debates | DISPUTES (J) |
| 28. idle talk; small talk | CHIT-CHAT (H) |
| 29. sharp; intense; penetrating; keen; incisive | ACUTE (J) |
| 30. as per written agreement or legal document | CONTRACTUAL (J) |
| 31. overpowering; staggering; crushing; irresistible | OVERWHELMING (I) |
| 32. images; idols | ICONS (J) |

## PART B

1. We refer again to the <u>SUPERSESSION</u> and primacy of international maritime law over corporate regulations.

2. The proposed amendments to the organization's charter have not yet been <u>SANCTIONED</u> by the board of governors, but their approval is expected within the week.

3. I simply mentioned, quite <u>INNOCUOUSLY</u> I thought, that Alice had put on a few extra pounds, at which point she threw the red wine in my face.

VOCABULARY WORK ANSWERS

4. Discovered by accident, Vivian Maier's ICONIC black and white images of American street life fascinate through both their pictorial narrative and the naturalness of the subjects she chose to depict.

5. In the hands of highly skilled performance musicians, musical instruments often EVOLVE into what seems to be a natural extension of the performer's body and mind.

6. We still need more time to carefully WEIGH the costs versus benefits of the project for our department.

7. By remaining silent throughout the prosecutor's questioning, Maria TACITLY acknowledged that her husband had committed the crime.

8. The regulations approved by the World Trade Organization in this matter SUPERSEDE all previously existing national statutes.

9. Although nothing was formalized in writing or in an actual verbal agreement, the TACIT assumption after days of negotiation was that corporate headquarters would cover our additional charges, which they're now refusing to do.

10. What was INITIALLY believed to be a severe cold actually turned out to be viral meningitis.

11. You are by no means OBLIGED to take my advice; it's simply intended as a suggestion.

12. A rarely cited CLAUSE in the state's penal code has been invoked to justify the severe punishment handed down by the court in its most recent case involving identity theft.

13. The country's entire tax system is CODIFIED in a three-thousand-page opus.

14. International disagreements involving unfair trading practices and currency manipulation are now routinely brought before the World Trade Organization's DISPUTE settlement body.

15. I'm afraid you are CONTRACTUALLY obliged to work every fifth Monday evening until 7:30 in addition to your regular 40-hour week.

16. Early childhood exposure to an avid reading environment is highly CORRELATED with later success in all areas of life.

UNIT THREE | DIFFERENT STROKES FOR DIFFERENT FOLKS

## PART C

> LANGUAGE FOCUS ANSWERS

1. Identify instances of grammatical parallelism in paragraphs A–C.

    i) *in terms of the forms of interaction the members of given societies engaged in, as well as the types of relationships typical of and expected within those cultures.*

    ii) *both the form and the content*

    iii) *the words, verb forms, and overall lexico-grammatical / lexico-pragmatic character*

    iv) *both Japanese and Korean*

    v) *lexical choice, word form, and syntax*

2. In paragraphs A–G, identify sentences that begin with prepositional phrases.

    i) *In high-context countries such as Japan and Korea, …*

    ii) *In Korean society …*

    iii) *In Japan …*

    iv) *At the workplace …*

    v) *In contrast …*

    vi) *In a rather humorous article …*

3. Identify the adverb clauses in paragraphs D–H and specify the type of adverb clauses used (e.g., causality, purpose, contrast, condition, etc.) [For a review of ADVERB CLAUSES, see the APPENDIX, section B.]

    i) *until the boss has left* [time]

    ii) *even if there is no such clause* [condition]

    iii) *if there is a tomorrow for her* [condition]

    iv) *because many aspects of individual conduct are codified in and sanctioned by contracts* [causality]

    v) *although the speakers harbor perhaps no hostile intentions at all* [concession]

    vi) *when / after the German parent company acquired the British carmaker Rover* [time]

    vii) *as the ship they're sailing on takes on water* [time]

    viii) *because they consider it "empty verbiage"* [causality]

    ix) *as Professor Juliane House … noted* [manner]

x) *as Evans noted* [manner]

xi) *when the two ran / bumped into each other at the train station* [time]

xii) *hence any translation of the congenial niceties ... meaningless* [effect]

4. In paragraph I, locate two reduced adverb clauses.

   i) *when uttered by a New Yorker*

   ii) *When spoken by a southerner*

5. What antecedent noun does the pronoun "she" refer to in the phrase "She might counter the chastising …" (paragraph E)?

   *A Berliner*

**Sentence Transformation**

6. Indra was the only daughter among five children, so her parents always gave priority to her brothers' wants and needs.

   **seat**

   Because Indra was the only daughter among five children, her own wants and needs always <u>took a back seat to</u> her brothers'.

7. The measures taken by the county government are unprecedented and demand an emergency meeting of the board of supervisors.

   **call**

   The unprecedented measures taken by the county government <u>call for an</u> emergency meeting of the board of supervisors.

8. When you're shopping for a new car, don't be fooled by cheap sales gimmicks.

   **taken**

   Don't allow yourself <u>to be taken in by</u> cheap sales gimmicks when you're shopping for a new car.

9. Monica and her husband frequently disagree over what type of food is best for their children.

   **odds**

   Monica and her husband are frequently <u>at odds (with each other) over</u> the best type of food to give their children.

10. When the largest donors pulled out their pledged funding, the project failed immediately.

**fell**

The project <u>fell through immediately</u> after the largest donors withdrew their pledged support.

## PART D

## Sentence Reconstruction

1. Communication styles in high-context cultures tend to be far less explicit than those found in low-context societies.

2. Berlin is described as a typical low-context city in which everyday speech patterns can appear to be very direct.

3. Relations between employers and employees in low-context cultures are largely determined by written contracts.

4. Relationships in high-context cultures normally evolve over a long time.

5. Individuals in low-context societies are less bound by tacit norms or codes of conduct.

6. In countries like Japan, individuals must consider the entire range of relations involved in a given situation before speaking or acting.

7. The English tend to rely on small talk to break the ice between individuals.

8. People in low power-distance cultures often feel that they are able to bring about desired changes in society.

9. Advertising campaigns in high-context cultures often place the individual in a group setting of friends or family members.

10. Multinational corporations have started to recognize the enormous importance of culturally mediated communication styles in the global workplace.

ULTIMATE CHALLENGE ANSWERS

# UNIT 4

# ENGLISH AS THE GLOBAL LINGUA FRANCA

## CLOZE TASK ANSWERS

CLOZE TASK / READING PASSAGE: Suggested answers [responses may vary].

[1] likened
[2] programming
[3] diplomacy
[4] consolidate / solidify
[5] endowments
[6] majority
[7] unnoticed
[8] competitors
[9] adaptation
[10] complexity
[11] grammatical
[12] receiver / recipient
[13] classification
[14] memorize / remember
[15] deciphering
[16] dramatically
[17] succession
[18] executives

[19] foreseeable
[20] geographic
[21] exceptionally
[22] comparison
[23] effective
[24] surpassing
[25] regionalization
[26] pronunciation
[27] immigrants
[28] widespread
[29] regionalized
[30] motivation
[31] intelligibility
[32] willingness
[33] exchanges
[34] substantial
[35] awareness
[36] overcome

# UNIT FOUR | ENGLISH AS THE GLOBAL LINGUA FRANCA

> VOCABULARY WORK ANSWERS

## PART A

| From Paragraphs A–H: | Synonymous Word or Phrase |
|---|---|
| 1. peers; equivalents in role; coequals; rivals; partners | COUNTERPARTS (E) |
| 2. portraying; describing; characterizing | DEPICTING (F) |
| 3. something that is easy; easy as pie | A PIECE OF CAKE (D) |
| 4. projects; ventures; operations; enterprises | UNDERTAKINGS (C) |
| 5. at the forefront; very advanced technologically | CUTTING-EDGE (B) |
| 6. eliminated; got rid of* | DONE AWAY WITH (E) |
| 7. eliminated; did away with* | DISPENSED WITH (E) |

*Responses in 6 and 7 are interchangeable

| | |
|---|---|
| 8. many-sided | MULTIFACETED (B) |
| 9. privilege or right; choice | PREROGATIVE (A) |
| 10. factual | DE FACTO (B) |
| 11. to make up; to compose | CONSTITUTE (B) |
| 12. hurdles; hindrances | OBSTACLES (C) |
| 13. required; binding; mandatory | OBLIGATORY (E) |
| 14. slimmed down in contour or profile; made less bulky | STREAMLINED (E) |
| 15. intimidating; extremely challenging | DAUNTING (C) |
| 16. gathered; composite; clustered; assembled | COLLECTIVE (C) |
| 17. of two tongues or languages | DIGLOSSIC (H) |
| 18. bombardment; profusion; plethora | BARRAGE (F) |
| 19. words that sound the same; words that are pronounced the same | HOMOPHONES (F) |
| 20. in an intimidating manner; arduously | FORMIDABLY (F) |
| 21. incomprehensible; indecipherable | UNINTELLIGIBLE (H) |

| From Paragraphs I–T: | Synonymous Word or Phrase |
|---|---|
| 22. tormenting; taunting; bedeviling | VEXING (J) |
| 23. augmented by; complemented by; strengthened; intensified by | ENHANCED (I) |
| 24. surpass in number | OUTNUMBER (K) |
| 25. probability | LIKELIHOOD (N) |
| 26. a district or county in New York City | BOROUGH (O) |
| 27. antiquated; obsolete; outdated | ARCHAIC (O) |
| 28. two or more vowel sounds spoken together as a gliding sound | DIPHTHONGS (O) |
| 29. fellow countrymen or countrywomen | COMPATRIOTS (N) |
| 30. be adequate; be enough; to fulfill | SUFFICE (K) |
| 31. uncompromising; intransigent; unyielding | DIE-HARD (K) |
| 32. of the highest order or rank; predominant; supreme; cardinal | PARAMOUNT (Q) |
| 33. reserved; quiet; taciturn; tight-lipped | RETICENT (Q) |
| 34. behavior; conduct | DEMEANOR (Q) |
| 35. to overcome the initial reserve between strangers; to engage in conversation | BREAK THE ICE (Q) |
| 36. rhythmic flow; beat | CADENCE (Q) |
| 37. aspects; sides | FACETS (R) |
| 38. be reluctant to do; be averse to do; be disinclined to do | SHY AWAY FROM (R) |
| 39. locating exactly; describing precisely | PINPOINTING (R) |

VOCABULARY WORK ANSWERS

PART B

1. In the United States, the <u>LIKELIHOOD</u> of an individual being killed by lightning is 30 times higher than that of being attacked by a shark.

2. Mysterious codes, texts, and scripts—such as Linear A, the Voynich Manuscript, the Indus Script, the Rohonc Codex, Rongorongo, and the Beale Ciphers—remain completely UNINTELLIGIBLE to cryptologists even today, despite many attempts to decipher the messages they contain.

3. Ship captains now use sophisticated radar and sonar equipment as early-warning systems for dangerous submarine OBSTACLES such as icebergs.

4. In most Japanese households, visitors are OBLIGED to remove their shoes before entering the host's apartment or house.

5. By and large, computer systems have DONE AWAY WITH the need for typewriters.

6. The vast majority of photographs created today are ENHANCED in some way using computer applications dedicated to the sophisticated manipulation of digital images.

7. It has always been the PREROGATIVE of the victors of armed conflicts to interpret and record the history of the circumstances and causes that led to war.

8. Frequent brushing and flossing are of PARAMOUNT importance for the maintenance of good oral hygiene.

9. For many individuals who suffer from depression, it is often difficult to PINPOINT any single, specific cause for their melancholy state of mind.

10. Poor computer skills are a major OBSTACLE for many who are trying to (re-)enter the workforce.

11. Despite hundreds of military and civilian photographs as well as thousands of eyewitness accounts, DIE-HARD skeptics are still unwilling to entertain the possibility that earth has been visited by UFOs.

12. German manufacturers of optical equipment have a long tradition of producing CUTTING-EDGE lens designs.

13. Despite his lifelong weak physical CONSTITUTION, Immanuel Kant lived to the ripe old age of 80.

14. Many renaissance paintings <u>DEPICT</u> scenes specifically requested by wealthy merchants or noblemen who had commissioned the works from individual artists.

15. Becoming a proficient speaker of any tone language such as Thai, Mandarin, Vietnamese, or Cantonese, is a <u>DAUNTING</u> task even for the most talented learners.

16. Picasso's <u>DEPICTION</u> of the bombing of the Spanish city of Guernica has become one of the most haunting representations of twentieth-century art.

> LANGUAGE FOCUS ANSWERS

## PART C

1. In paragraph A, find pronouns used as sentence subjects.

   *neither; both*

2. Identify instances of grammatical parallelism in paragraph B.

   *in international trade, finance, science, technology, transportation, and diplomacy; The economic, scientific, and technological strength of the United States; on land, on the seas, and in the air.*

3. In paragraphs B–D, identify present participles used as adjectives. [Note that present participles and gerunds have the same grammatical form but different syntactic functions, e.g., eating, writing, working, walking, etc.]

   *leading universities; cutting-edge research; promising careers; daunting*

4. In paragraphs D–F, find adverbs that modify adjectives. Find the passive verb phrases used in paragraphs K–N and identify their tense. [For a review of the PASSIVE VOICE, see the APPENDIX, section F.]

   Adverbs that modify adjectives:

   *extraordinarily difficult; highly dynamic; equally complex; extraordinarily complex; highly inflecting; quite unnecessary; much easier; formidably difficult*

   Passive verb phrases:

   *encountered at international conferences* [present simple in the reduced relative clause]

   *conducted by native speakers* [present simple in the reduced relative clause] *held by India and the United States* [present simple in the reduced relative clause]

*was also frequently associated with* [past simple]

*might be noted* [modal + present simple passive infinitive without "to"]

*not held* [present simple in the reduced relative clause]

5. In paragraphs K and L, identify the simple subjects in each sentence, i.e., the subject that agrees with the finite sentence verb.

   i)   *comparison*
   ii)  *interactions*
   iii) *middle class*
   iv)  *efforts*
   v)   *Li Yang*
   vi)  *China*
   vii) *China*

### Sentence Transformation

6. Many people are simply unfit for stressful jobs.

   **cut**

   Many people <u>are simply not cut out for</u> extremely stressful jobs.

7. Several of us were quite annoyed at Timothy when he refused to help us with the first draft of our proposal.

   **off**

   Several of us were quite <u>put off by Timothy's</u> refusal to help us with the first draft of our proposal.

8. The company CEO went out of his way to make light of the firm's third-quarter loss.

   **play**

   The company CEO went out of his way <u>to play down</u> the firm's third-quarter loss.

9. If you put in one additional hour per day over the next eight days, you can compensate for the day you were absent.

   **make**

   You <u>can make up for</u> the day you were absent if you put in one additional hour per day over the next eight days.

10. Most of the problems the firm is experiencing can be attributed to poor management.

**boil**

Most of the problems the firm is experiencing <u>boil down to</u> poor management.

## ULTIMATE CHALLENGE ANSWERS

## PART D

### Sentence Reconstruction

1. Scientists who are unable to communicate in English are at a distinct disadvantage when it comes to getting published in peer-reviewed journals.

2. Non-native speakers of English greatly outnumber native speakers.

3. Unlike the nominal systems of highly inflecting languages, English nouns do not have gender.

4. All words in Mandarin Chinese are characterized by one of four possible tones.

5. Standard Arabic displays an extremely complex system of grammar based on word roots consisting of three consonants.

6. Tseze is given as an example of a language that has obligatory evidentiary markings.

7. Hindi and Urdu present very challenging phonological problems for Western learners of the languages.

8. In many cultures, some form of feedback is an essential feature of successful communication.

9. Motivation and ability play important roles in the acquisition of a second language.

10. Even within the same English-speaking country, there are often wide regional variations in pronunciation.

# SOCIAL NETWORKS AND THE REVOLUTION IN COMMUNICATION

UNIT 5

CLOZE TASK / READING PASSAGE: Suggested answers [responses may vary].

CLOZE TASK ANSWERS

[1] way
[2] know
[3] if
[4] unfold / happen / develop
[5] events
[6] times
[7] share
[8] resources / tools / instruments
[9] clients / customers / users
[10] company / corporate
[11] concerns / questions
[12] industry / profession
[13] opportunity / chance
[14] engaged / involved
[15] side(s)
[16] posted
[17] admit / allow
[18] applicants
[19] edition
[20] hired
[21] personal
[22] set
[23] need
[24] so
[25] themselves
[26] out
[27] filed / brought
[28] see / experience / discover
[29] develops / happens / unfolds / evolves
[30] reach
[31] allowing / enabling

# VOCABULARY WORK ANSWERS

## PART A

| From Paragraphs A–G: | Synonymous Word or Phrase |
|---|---|
| 1. scenes or reels from a motion picture | FOOTAGE (C) |
| 2. restoration; renewal; reparation; mending; amelioration | REHABILITATION (F) |
| 3. mentally, psychologically, or emotionally overwhelming | MIND-BOGGLING (B) |
| 4. privacy; closeness to another in a private manner | INTIMACY (G) |
| 5. penetrated; passed into; filtered into | PERMEATED (F) |
| 6. pathway; approach; route | CHANNEL (D) |
| 7. an entity of gigantic size | BEHEMOTH (A) |
| 8. soared; climbed; shot up | ROCKETED (B) |
| 9. defeating; besting; surmounting | OVERCOMING (F) |
| 10. holding; possessing; sporting; flaunting | BOASTING (B) |
| 11. disseminated; spread out | SCATTERED (F) |
| 12. misleadingly; illusively | DECEPTIVELY (G) |
| 13. gained an advantage from; profited from | BENEFITED (E) |
| 14. violence; rebellion; uprising; uproar | TURMOIL (C) |
| 15. popular; in demand | HOT (D) |
| 16. deserve; justify; call for | WARRANT (C) |
| 17. poignant; acute; intense; deep in meaning | PROFOUND (A) |
| 18. premiere; initial appearance; launch; beginning | DEBUT (B) |

| From Paragraphs H–T: | Synonymous Word or Phrase |
|---|---|
| 19. offhand; offhanded; cursory; loose; informal | CASUAL (I) |
| 20. shrewdly informed or aware of; canny | SAVVY (M) |
| 21. saddening; distressing | DISHEARTENING (J) |
| 22. to screen or filter out | TO WEED OUT (H) |
| 23. spotlessly; perfectly; flawlessly | IMPECCABLY (H) |
| 24. tempting; beguiling; inciting; exciting; stimulating | PROVOCATIVE (H) |
| 25. through; by means of | VIA (L) |
| 26. pure and acceptable for consumption by Jews; legitimate | KOSHER (M) |
| 27. unaware; off guard; trusting; credulous | UNSUSPECTING (I) |
| 28. finished; refined; cultured; genteel; perfected | POLISHED (H) |
| 29. elicit; bring out; draw out | COAX OUT (L) |
| 30. emerging; appearing | SURFACING (M) |
| 31. clothes; dress; apparel | ATTIRE (H) |
| 32. nose-dived | PLUMMETED (M) |
| 33. in dispute; debatable; moot; open to doubt; controversial | QUESTIONABLE (M) |
| 34. a collection of files or documents pertaining to a topic or person | DOSSIER (I) |
| 35. sexually enticing or provocative | RACY (H) |
| 36. improvement | BETTERMENT (T) |
| 37. usual; ordinary; mundane; general; run-of-the-mill | COMMONPLACE (J) |

## VOCABULARY WORK ANSWERS

### PART B

1. The now-retired American spy plane, SR 71—also known as "Black Bird"—made its service <u>DEBUT</u> in 1964.

2. Garlic, turmeric, pumpkin, ginger, and fish oil have been shown to be very <u>BENEFICIAL</u> to patients suffering from various forms of chronic inflammation.

3. The "Zapruder film," which is <u>FOOTAGE</u> taken of the actual assassination of U.S. President John F. Kennedy as the killing unfolded, has become one of the most renowned pieces of documentary film ever recorded.

4. Frankly, in our view, the negative ad hominem attacks our opponent has launched in his candidacy do not even <u>WARRANT</u> a response.

5. Franz Kafka's novels and short stories portray deeply thought-<u>PROVOKING</u> motifs and plots in which individuals become trapped in impossible circumstances and arcane bureaucratic labyrinths.

6. Upon the death of North Korean leader Kim Jung Il, television broadcasts showed thousands of North Korean citizens completely <u>OVERCOME</u> with emotion.

7. News of the collapse of New York investment giant Lehman Brothers sent stock markets <u>PLUMMETING</u> worldwide, with the Dow Jones index shaving off more than 770 points in a single day.

8. With its vast resources of tools and information covering essentially the entire spectrum of human knowledge, the Internet has <u>PROFOUNDLY</u> affected the way we live, work, play, date, and otherwise relate to our entire planet.

9. Job applicants are always advised to <u>POLISH</u> their CVs and resumes before sending out application packages.

10. Unfortunately, those conducting the interview felt that Paul was simply too <u>CASUALLY</u> dressed for the occasion; in fact, he was reportedly even wearing a T-shirt.

11. One of the most famous Latin expressions still used today reads: cui bono?—or in English: who <u>BENEFITS</u>, or who stands to gain?

UNIT FIVE | SOCIAL NETWORKS AND THE REVOLUTION IN COMMUNICATION

12. I was astonished that the director was offended by what I thought was nothing more than a CASUAL comment about the weather.

13. The use of cell phones and their many applications is so COMMONPLACE today that many people don't know how they would survive without them.

14. News of the tragedy didn't SURFACE until the responsible agencies had double-checked all the facts, and even then the spokespersons were anything but forthcoming with details.

15. SAVVY tax accountants can exploit every possible loophole in the existing tax laws to save their clients as much money as is legally possible.

16. The use of capital punishment as a crime deterrent is highly QUESTIONABLE and does not appear to be supported by factual evidence.

## PART C

1. Identify the complete sentence subjects in each sentence in paragraphs B and C.

> i) *social networks and social media*
> ii) *Facebook*
> iii) *Facebook*
> iv) *the outside world*
> v) *Cell phones equipped with cameras of even moderate resolution*
> vi) *the entire world*
> vii) *citizens in strife-torn areas*
> viii) *users*

LANGUAGE FOCUS ANSWERS

2. Identify instances of sentence inversion in paragraphs I and J. [For a review of sentence INVERSION, see the APPENDIX, section E.]

> *Of perhaps even greater concern is the potential for identity theft, …* [The opening prepositional phrase requires sentence inversion.]
>
> *Particularly disheartening and worrisome is a trend …* [Inversion is used for strong emphasis.]

3. Find the passive verb phrases used in paragraphs K–M and identify their tense. [For a review of the PASSIVE VOICE, see the APPENDIX, section F.]

*may be used* [modal + simple present passive infinitive without "to"]

*was once asked* [past passive]

*was first reported* [past passive]

*and later confirmed* [subordinated past passive from the previous "was first reported …]

*were seen* [past passive]

4. What antecedent noun does the pronoun "its" refer to in the phrase "… on display in its best behavior" (paragraph H)?

*public persona*

5. What would be a synonymous expression for "strife-torn areas" in paragraph C?

*war zones; regions experiencing (civil) unrest / conflict / upheaval*

**Sentence Transformation**

6. This performance setback is attributable to the team's lack of preparation and practice.
**chalked**
The team's poor performance can <u>be chalked up to</u> a lack of preparation and practice.

7. The new tax laws have largely eliminated government audits.
**done**
The new tax laws have largely <u>done away with</u> government audits.

8. David is simply not capable of leading this team.
**task**
David is simply not <u>up to the task of</u> leading this team.

9. At this rate, it's impossible to predict how long construction of the new wing will take.
**telling**
At this rate, there's <u>no telling how long</u> construction of the new wing will take.

10. The board of directors insist that they were absolutely clueless that a hostile takeover was being attempted.

**whatsoever**

The board of directors insist that they had <u>no clue / no idea / no knowledge whatsoever</u> that a hostile takeover was being attempted.

## PART D

### Sentence Reconstruction

1. Social media sites connect hundreds of millions of people throughout the world.

2. Social networking sites have increased the participatory role of civil society in shaping public policies.

3. People who are suffering from a wide range of afflictions can find immediate support in dedicated online forums.

4. Clear-cut boundaries between what is public and what is private appear to be vanishing as a result of the integration of social media into our daily lives.

5. Many companies use sophisticated data mining software to screen job applicants' entries on social networking sites.

6. Victims of identity theft are often lured into providing key details about their personal history to members of online forums.

7. Companies have become increasingly aware of the importance of the feedback provided by customers on social networking sites.

8. Families of the critically ill are able to provide real-time updates on the condition of the patient.

9. Patients who are recuperating from illness or injury often use social media to provide their friends and family with real-time updates on their progress.

10. The English language itself has been affected by the widespread popularity of social networking sites.

> ULTIMATE CHALLENGE ANSWERS

# UNIT 6

# MONEY MAKES THE WORLD GO ROUND

## CLOZE TASK ANSWERS

CLOZE TASK / READING PASSAGE: Suggested answers [responses may vary].

[1] irrespective
[2] monetary
[3] globalization
[4] percentage
[5] wealthiest
[6] exception(s)
[7] variation
[8] liability
[9] recipients / receivers
[10] electronically
[11] presumably
[12] additional
[13] borrower
[14] payments
[15] founder
[16] movement
[17] industrial
[18] supplier
[19] embodied
[20] unsustainable
[21] economists
[22] indebted
[23] heavily
[24] calamitous
[25] tumultuous
[26] withdrew
[27] insolvent
[28] liquidity
[29] necessitate
[30] industrialized

# UNIT SIX | MONEY MAKES THE WORLD GO ROUND

## VOCABULARY WORK ANSWERS

## PART A

From Paragraphs A–H:    Synonymous Word or Phrase

1. direct; on target; exactly on a topic    POINT BLANK (C)
2. simple; open; aboveboard; up front; no-nonsense; plain    STRAIGHTFORWARD (F)
3. amass; collect; accumulate    ACCRUE (G)
4. satisfy debts; settle a debt in full    PAY OFF (G)
5. indigence; destitution    POVERTY (B)
6. completing as a final element or item in a list    ROUNDING OUT (B)
7. circulates; spreads; disseminates    DISPERSES (F)
8. greater part; lion's share    BULK (E)
9. believability; reliability; trustworthiness    CREDIBILITY (D)
10. in an instant and without preparation    AT A MOMENT'S NOTICE (A)
11. dropping off; waning; declining    SLIPPING (B)
12. booking; recording; earning    LOGGING IN (B)
13. entering a position; crossing a threshold or mark    COMING IN (B)
14. being last in a hopeless position    LEFT OUT IN THE COLD (H)

From Paragraphs I–P:    Synonymous Word or Phrase

15. earn; gain; procure; acquire; come into    REAP (K)
16. the basic level; the primary part    GRASSROOTS (J)
17. destroyed to a great extent    DECIMATED (K)
18. size; measure; degree; extent    MAGNITUDE (L)
19. novelty; creating new things or methods    INNOVATION (K)
20. monetary shortfalls    DEFICITS (L)

| | |
|---|---|
| 21. consequence; effect; influence | IMPACT (K) |
| 22. peak; summit; acme; zenith | PINNACLE (L) |
| 23. advisors; leaders in a particular field; mentors | GURUS (M) |
| 24. the fundamental framework of a community, area, or country, including utilities, transportation, etc. | INFRASTRUCTURE (J) |
| 25. debilitated; weakened; impaired | CRIPPLED (K) |
| 26. full force or impact; effects; consequences | BRUNT (P) |
| 27. fantasy; illusion | PIPE DREAM (O) |
| 28. to support; to buttress; to prop up | SHORE UP (N) |
| 29. horrible; awful; dreadful; alarming; grim | DIRE (N) |

VOCABULARY WORK ANSWERS

PART B

1. Because of an 18% rise in imports from OPEC countries and a 22% increase in imports of consumer goods from the Far East, the U.S. current account DEFICIT has now reached unsustainable levels.

2. With government deficits running at record-high levels in almost all Western countries, the socioeconomic outlook for many fixed-income retirees is indeed DIRE, and fears are mounting that vast numbers of senior citizens will simply be unable to live on their own in the future or to receive the proper medical care they will require.

3. Communities and states that have found themselves deep in debt have simply been unable to afford major INFRASTRUCTURE projects such as repaving crumbling roads, replacing sagging, corroded bridges, or bolstering giant above-ground parking facilities.

4. Truth be told, banks simply do not want debtors to PAY OFF their loans in the shortest time possible because that would prevent the lenders from earning the compound interest they would otherwise receive.

5. Criticized by many economists as unacceptably low, the official POVERTY rate in the United States as of 2012 is defined as a four-person-household annual income of $23,050.

6. People from low-context cultures tend to have a very frank, often uncomfortably STRAIGHTFORWARD style of communicating.

7. Estimates predict that the IMPACT of a one-mile-wide asteroid with the Pacific Ocean would send a 500-meter wall of water racing eastward as far as Dallas, Texas, destroying virtually everything in its path; the effect would be nearly identical for all nations bordering the western rim of the ocean.

8. Visual displays have benefited tremendously from INNOVATIVE designs using organic light-emitting diodes.

9. Tennis legend Steffi Graf reached the PINNACLE of her career with her 1999 victory over young Martina Hingis at the French Open tournament in Paris.

10. In many societies around the world, women still do not REAP the same monetary rewards as their male counterparts for an equal or greater quantity of work.

11. Patterns of emigration feature similarities across continents and ages, with persecuted, IMPOVERISHED masses seeking a more humane and financially stable life in greener pastures abroad.

12. As INCREDIBLE as it may seem, the two young girls were able to contort their bodies into a clear acrylic box of only nine cubic feet.

13. Having now been shown to have lied on at least three occasions during his testimony, the prosecution's star witness has lost all CREDIBILITY in our view.

14. The BRUNT force of the iceberg impact tore a gaping hole into the starboard bow of the Titanic.

15. Your balance of principal plus ACCRUED interest stands at $275,000.00.

16. Residents in the coastal regions of Indonesia, the Philippines, Taiwan, and Japan, must be ready AT A MOMENT'S NOTICE to move to higher ground following an earthquake.

## LANGUAGE FOCUS ANSWERS

PART C

1. Identify all FIRST CONDITIONALS in paragraphs A–I. [For a review of CONDITIONALS, see the APPENDIX, section G.]

   *If, for example, the government sells debt (bonds) in the amount of $10 billion and the government account is credited with that same amount in the Federal Reserve's banking system, …*

2. Identify all ZERO CONDITIONALS in paragraphs A–I.

   *When it comes right down to it, …*
   *… when they see it, …*
   *When asked point blank, …*
   *When the U.S. government needs money, …*
   *When entire countries are the recipients of loans, …*

3. Identify all SECOND CONDITIONALS in paragraphs A–I.

   *If the borrower surprisingly paid off the entire amount within two months, …*
   *… for if they did …*

4. Find instances of noun apposition in paragraphs A and B. [An example of apposition: *Khalid, a student from Baghdad, arrived in Sydney on July 10.*]

   *… the jet-setters who can fly off to their own private island …*
   *… computer whiz and Harvard dropout, Bill Gates, founder of Microsoft.*

5. What antecedent noun does the pronoun "it" refer to in the phrase "The answer of course is that it isn't!" in paragraph H?

   the money … to pay off the interest

### Sentence Transformation

6. News of the coup attempt quickly went viral.
   **wildfire**
   News of the coup attempt <u>spread like wildfire</u>.

7. Despite my mother's ripe old age of 97, she stays informed of all the latest news.
   **abreast**
   Despite my mother's ripe old age of 97, she <u>keeps abreast of / stays abreast of</u> all the latest news.

8. Luckily, we had developed the delegation's itinerary well ahead of time.

**worked**

Luckily, we had worked out the delegation's itinerary well ahead of time.

9. I'm happy to say that both our children passed their medical license exams with highest marks.
   **colors**
   I'm happy to say that both our children passed their medical license exams with flying colors.

10. We managed to install the new operating system with no problem at all.
    **hitch**
    We managed to install the new operating system without a hitch.

PART D

Sentence Reconstruction

1. Globalization has brought about massive shifts in the distribution of wealth and poverty.

2. In much of the world, money comes into being through a banking mechanism known as the money multiplier.

3. Commercial banks create out of thin air ninety percent of the money in circulation.

4. When the US government needs money, it must sell certificates of debt to the nation's central bank in exchange for an electronic check.

5. The U.S. dollar is based on debt and is backed by nothing more than the government's promise to pay.

6. Treasury notes are nothing more than the government's promise to pay back the amount designated by the denomination of the note plus accrued interest.

7. China and Russia have far more billionaires and millionaires today than either country had twenty years ago.

8. Today, Asia is home to eight out of ten of the world's wealthiest countries.

9. In a public banking system, the interest earned by the lender on commercial loans is directed back into public coffers.

10. It is in the banks' best interest for borrowers to remain in debt until loans reach their full maturity.

ULTIMATE CHALLENGE ANSWERS

# UNIT 7

# STOCKS, BONDS, AND WHAT WENT WRONG

## CLOZE TASK ANSWERS

CLOZE TASK / READING PASSAGE: Suggested answers [responses may vary].

[1] way / approach / method
[2] problem
[3] drawback / downside / disadvantage
[4] stands
[5] line / accordance
[6] calculated / determined / measured / set / established
[7] too
[8] underestimating
[9] differ
[10] whereas / while
[11] constitute / represent
[12] turn
[13] history / life spans
[14] fall
[15] reaches

[16] issued
[17] converted
[18] out
[19] both
[20] which
[21] maturity
[22] gains / profits / rewards
[23] research
[24] end
[25] cash
[26] basis
[27] shareholders
[28] bonds
[29] cooked / dreamed
[30] done / conducted
[31] these
[32] up

UNIT SEVEN | STOCKS, BONDS, AND WHAT WENT WRONG

[33] acronym
[34] again
[35] money
[36] effect
[37] process
[38] multiplied
[39] uncovered / revealed
[40] sums
[41] out

[42] levels
[43] become
[44] both
[45] lay
[46] which
[47] out
[48] fill
[49] law
[50] that

## VOCABULARY WORK ANSWERS

## PART A

From the reading text, find the words or phrases that have similar meanings to the words / phrases given in the numbered lists below. The first one has been done for you as an example.

From Paragraphs A–J:                        Synonymous Word or Phrase

1. center; middle; heart                    CORE (B)
2. believed; thought; held to be; presumed  DEEMED (B)
3. erratic; changeable; unstable            VOLATILE (B)
4. liquidate; turn into money; exchange     CASH IN (B)
5. sudden increases in price or value       SPIKES (B)
6. monitors (verb); keeps informed of;
   stays abreast of                         TRACKS (B)
7. revenue; profit; income                  EARNINGS (A)
8. excited; vehement; passionate; worked-up HEATED (D)
9. insolvency; ruin; failure                BANKRUPTCY (C)
10. a catastrophic collapse of the core elements
    of something                            MELTDOWN (D)
11. drawback; disadvantage                  DOWNSIDE (F)
12. a trading period in stocks characterized by
    falling share prices                    BEAR MARKET (H)
13. a trading period in stocks characterized by
    rising share prices                     BULL MARKET (H)

| | |
|---|---|
| 14. fail; die out (as a business) | GO BELLY UP (F) |
| 15. supporters; advocates; promoters | SPONSORS (J) |
| 16. climax; conclusion; end result; closing | CULMINATION (J) |
| 17. glaring; unmistakable; plain; patent; evident | STARK (J) |
| 18. specifications; stipulations; terms; clauses; conditions | PROVISIONS (J) |
| 19. revoked; rescinded; reversed; overturned | REPEALED (J) |
| 20. periods of inflated market prices for specific items or commodities based largely on speculation | BUBBLES (I) |
| 21. real; concrete; touchable; physical | TANGIBLE (I) |
| 22. authorization; empowerment | ENTITLEMENT (G) |
| 23. sell-off of a company's assets, for example in a bankruptcy | LIQUIDATION (G) |

| From Paragraphs K–T: | Synonymous Word or Phrase |
|---|---|
| 24. a bet; a gamble | WAGER (L) |
| 25. tiers or ranks in command or hierarchy | ECHELONS (K) |
| 26. at the edge of a steep drop or at a critical juncture | BRINK (L) |
| 27. an extreme height; a layer of the earth's atmosphere | STRATOSPHERE (N) |
| 28. deceitful tricks; mischievous deeds | SHENANIGANS (N) |
| 29. trash; worthless garbage | JUNK (M) |
| 30. reputedly; supposedly; allegedly | OSTENSIBLY (O) |
| 31. annihilated; destroyed; wiped out | OBLITERATED (O) |
| 32. traded in exchange | BARTERED (M) |
| 33. the top level; the top layer | CREAM (M) |
| 34. crooked; dishonest; criminal; shady | FRAUDULENT (M) |
| 35. restore; refill; re-supply | REPLENISH (N) |
| 36. paid for (often unhappily); handed over | FORKED OVER (S) |
| 37. funds; a treasury | COFFERS (S) |
| 38. extra money (besides salary) given to an employee who is leaving a company | SEVERANCE PAY (Q) |

39. cutting back; reducing; decreasing — CURTAILING (O)

40. leery; wary; distrustful; doubting — SUSPICIOUS (T)

**VOCABULARY WORK ANSWERS**

## PART B

1. When businesses GO BELLY UP, their assets and inventories are often liquidated at fire sale prices, creating welcome buying opportunities for bargain hunters.

2. The MELTDOWN of the core of a nuclear reactor constitutes one of the most serious and potentially lethal catastrophes in any country, with long-term effects from radioactive fallout that transcend all national boundaries.

3. Many western banks and other corporations have received strong public criticism for rewarding their parting CEOs with hefty bonuses and SEVERANCE packages that are, by all rational standards, simply obscene.

4. For most people, the STARK differences between the lifestyles of billionaires and those of homeless street people are almost impossible to imagine.

5. Historically, realistic threats of military conflict in the Persian Gulf have caused oil prices to SPIKE.

6. After thorough investigation and research trials at a number of medical centers all across the U.S., the claims made by a fairly prominent cancer specialist that he had discovered an extremely effective novel form of treatment were found to be FRAUDULENT.

7. Although their true purpose may never be known, the giant stone statues that face out to sea from various points on Easter Island were OSTENSIBLY erected to ward off potential invaders arriving by boat.

8. Within days after the United States Supreme Court allowed most of President Obama's national health care law to stand, the president's political opponents vowed to REPEAL the law in Congress.

9. One of the major DOWNSIDES to living in dense urban environments is having to breathe very unhealthy air.

10. Having just lost his job and his home, John was pushed to the BRINK of an emotional breakdown when his wife filed for divorce.

11. After the global financial crisis of 2008, many individuals and companies lost substantial amounts of their net worth and assets, forcing many into BANKRUPTCY proceedings.

12. When markets turn sour, many investors often decide to CASH IN their portfolios, or, in other words, to take the money and run.

13. Gymnast Nadia Comaneci's first-ever scores of perfect 10s during the 1976 Montreal Olympics were the CULMINATION of extraordinary talent, steely nerves, phenomenal perseverance, countless hours of training, and an insatiable pursuit of perfection.

14. The mass exodus of wealthier citizens and businesses out of southern California will likely CULMINATE in substantially reduced tax revenue for the region.

15. The new trade agreement does not include PROVISIONS for renegotiating labor disputes that will likely arise as a result of outsourcing.

16. Significant PROVISIONS of the armistice agreement ending World War I dealt with the issue of reparations demanded by France and Great Britain from Germany.

LANGUAGE FOCUS ANSWERS

PART C

1. Find instances of ZERO CONDITIONALS in paragraphs A–D.

    i)   *When states, companies, or other corporate entities need to raise money, …*

    ii)  *… when transportation costs rise as a result of geopolitical turmoil and spikes in oil prices, …*

2. Find instances of FIRST CONDITIONALS in paragraphs E–F.

    i)   *if interest rates fall below the rates that were in play at the time the bond was originally issued.*

    ii)  *if the company's market value goes up.*

3. In paragraphs G–J, find instances of identifying / defining relative clauses.

    i)    *who invest in the stock market*
    ii)   *the holder has to regular dividends* [reduced relative clause]
    iii)  *that become extremely profitable*
    iv)   *traded in stocks* [reduced relative clause]
    v)    *who have been burned by falling stock prices in a bear market*

UNIT SEVEN | STOCKS, BONDS, AND WHAT WENT WRONG

vi) *Cooked up / Dreamed up in the brains of "Quantz wizards,"* [reduced relative clause placed pre-positional to the subject of the sentence]

vii) *Named after its original sponsors, Senator Carter Glass and Representative Henry Steagall,* [reduced relative clause placed pre-positional to the subject of the sentence]

viii) *Through which they could finance their operations* [this relative clause modifies the antecedent noun "means"]

4. In paragraphs G–J, find instances of non-identifying / non-defining relative clauses.

i) *which give the buyer voting rights in the company.*
ii) *which sent stocks into atmospheric bubbles, …*
iii) *which was also known as the "Banking Act."*

5. What antecedent noun does the pronoun "they" refer to at the end of the first sentence in paragraph M ". . . they didn't."

*these vast sums of illusionary money*

**Sentence Transformation**

6. I'm not sure if these shoes are the right size. May I wear them to see if they fit?

**try**

I'm not sure if these shoes are the right size. May I <u>try them on</u> to see if they fit?

7. Cynthia must have eaten something that didn't agree with her because she's been vomiting for the last two hours.

**up**

Cynthia must have eaten something that didn't agree with her because she's <u>been throwing up</u> for the last two hours.

8. My husband is using several social media sites to find the whereabouts of his high school classmates.

**down**

My husband is using several social media sites <u>to track down</u> his high school classmates.

9. Your sister has come through the operation very successfully but she's still in critical condition.

**woods**

Your sister has come through the operation very successfully but she's <u>not out of the woods</u> yet.

10. I think Ian simply made the spontaneous decision to invite his bad-tempered neighbors to the block party without considering the consequences.

**spur**

I think Ian simply decided on <u>the spur of the moment</u> to invite his bad-tempered neighbors to the block party without considering the consequences.

## ULTIMATE CHALLENGE ANSWERS

### PART D

### Sentence Reconstruction

1. Common stocks usually give shareholders voting rights in a company whereas preferred stocks do not.

2. When a company is forced into liquidation, bondholders must be paid out first, followed by shareholders of preferred stock.

3. The U.S. government excludes food and energy prices from the measures it uses to calculate rates of inflation.

4. County and state governments in the USA regularly issue municipal bonds to fund desired infrastructure projects.

5. The volume of trading in bonds is roughly three times greater than that of stocks.

6. Stocks and bonds normally stand in an inverse relationship to each other in terms of demand.

7. Staggering sums of money were created and lost through elaborate investment schemes involving derivatives such as credit default swaps.

8. At the height of the US housing bubble, bankers were encouraged to issue mortgage loans even to people with no source of income.

9. In response to the economic crisis of 2008, thousands of lending institutions froze their credit lines.

10. Businesses that no longer had access to credit with which to purchase needed supplies and services were forced to close their doors.

# ALPHA CITIES AND MEGACITIES

UNIT 8

CLOZE TASK / READING PASSAGE: Suggested answers [responses may vary].

[1] settlements
[2] continuously
[3] intolerable
[4] industrialization
[5] undreamed / undreamt
[6] surroundings
[7] survival
[8] immortalized
[9] administrative
[10] exponential
[11] connectivity
[12] indicative
[13] architectural
[14] encompasses
[15] unstoppable
[16] imbalances
[17] governance
[18] increasingly
[19] characterized
[20] outskirts
[21] protected
[22] robberies
[23] extortion
[24] inhabitants
[25] enlightening

CLOZE TASK ANSWERS

## PART A

| From Paragraphs A–I: | Synonymous Word or Phrase |
|---|---|
| 1. give and take; mutuality; interchange | RECIPROCITY (E) |
| 2. shrewdness to survive or succeed in any kind of environment or situation | STREET SMARTS (F) |

VOCABULARY WORK ANSWERS

| | | |
|---|---|---|
| 3. | periods lasting 1,000 years | MILLENNIA (B) |
| 4. | an object or tool made by human beings | ARTIFACT (B) |
| 5. | persistence; perseverance; endurance; stamina | TENACITY (F) |
| 6. | misfortunes; difficulties; adverse circumstances | HARDSHIPS (C) |
| 7. | prototypical; being the perfect embodiment of something | QUINTESSENTIAL (C) |
| 8. | groups; aggregates; collections | CLUSTERS (B) |
| 9. | perfect model or ideal of something | PARAGON (C) |
| 10. | vast plains of grasslands | STEPPES (C) |
| 11. | of prominent, high rank or importance | EMINENT (H) |
| 12. | drainage pipes or channels for waste water and refuse | SEWERS (H) |
| 13. | flight or departure from a place, often on a mass scale; emigration | EXODUS (G) |
| 14. | a person or firm with an advisory function | CONSULTANCY (I) |
| 15. | focal points; centers of activity; convergence points | HUBS (G) |

| From Paragraphs J–U: | Synonymous Word or Phrase |
|---|---|
| 16. stressed; highlighted; emphasized | ACCENTUATED (J) |
| 17. budding; beginning; developing | NASCENT (L) |
| 18. imparities; inequalities | DISPARITIES (P) |
| 19. the condition or state of being placed side by side | JUXTAPOSITION (Q) |
| 20. extensive; inclusive; expansive | COMPREHENSIVE (P) |
| 21. workable; practicable | VIABLE (Q) |
| 22. clusters; groups; collections | AGGLOMERATIONS (O) |
| 23. dirty; miserably degraded; foul | SQUALID (S) |
| 24. an inkling; a flicker; a twinkle | GLIMMER (T) |
| 25. a container of explosive material; (figuratively: a potentially explosive situation) | POWDER KEG (S) |
| 26. invoke | CONJURE UP (S) |

# UNIT EIGHT | ALPHA CITIES AND MEGACITIES

27. money paid to kidnappers in exchange for a person or thing of value — RANSOM (Q)

28. lacking means for food and clothing; impoverished — DESTITUTE (Q)

29. criminal domains of society — UNDERWORLD (Q)

30. famous in a negative way; infamous; disreputable; ill-famed — NOTORIOUS (R)

## PART B

1. Until well after the time of Newton, Aristotelian logic served as the PARAGON of deductive reasoning.

2. The HARDSHIPS endured by many of the families of the Dust Bowl era are touchingly recounted in John Steinbeck's *The Grapes of Wrath*.

3. With extremely poor eyesight, bats rely on a greatly HEIGHTENED sense of hearing and an elaborate internal system of echolocation for survival.

4. Tennis legend Monica Seles enjoyed a reputation for being one of the most TENACIOUS players ever to master the game, playing every single point as if it was match point and never giving her opponents any reprieve from a seemingly endless series of blasted groundstrokes.

5. What is believed to be the world's oldest toilet and SEWAGE / SEWER system dating back to 764 BCE was unearthed in the Turkish province of Van.

6. High-end digital cameras of 50 MP and more have established themselves as VIABLE alternatives to traditional film cameras and as particularly flexible instruments in the hands of professional photographers.

7. Born to an inmate mother in Newgate prison, Daniel Dafoe's title character Moll Flanders not only survived in London through her beguiling charm and wily STREET SMARTS, but also went on to become impressively wealthy.

8. Financial CONSULTANTS advise clients on a wide range of investment options to protect and expand the client's wealth.

9. Instead of treating isolated, specific symptoms of illness, holistic medicine adopts a COMPREHENSIVE approach to the biological body as a functional whole.

VOCABULARY WORK ANSWERS

10. During the Dust Bowl era of the 1930s, many of America's farmers were left <u>DESTITUTE</u> as the relentless drought turned their once fertile farmland into barren dust, forcing thousands of families into homelessness and hunger.

11. <u>NOTORIOUS</u> for his apparently insatiable sexual drive, Mongolian conqueror Genghis Khan passed on his genes to an estimated 16 million descendants.

12. In everyday dealings with others, individuals in collectivist agricultural societies tend to rely on long-standing traditions of <u>RECIPROCATION / RECIPROCITY</u> rather than on codified prescriptive contracts.

13. Pictures of the Great Pyramids of Giza always <u>CONJURE UP</u> images of Cleopatra, King Tut, and a host of other iconic symbols of the once great ancient civilization.

14. Different types of industrial/technological research and development centers tend to occur in <u>CLUSTERS</u> in various countries, such as information technology centers in Boston and Silicon Valley in the USA; Hsinchu Science Park in Taiwan; Samsung Town in Seoul, South Korea; Kansai Science City in Japan; Bangalore in India; Dalian Hi-Tech Zone and Jiaxing Software Park in China; the Technologie Zentrum Chemnitz and the Dresden Centers of computer technology in Germany; and in dozens of decentralized research centers spread throughout France and other countries.

15. Texas-based radio host Alex Jones gained widespread <u>NOTORIETY</u> for his vehement opposition to globalization in almost every form.

16. When school children disrupt normal classroom instruction or become aggressive or violent, counselors and psychologists usually bring in the parents of the students for <u>CONSULTATION(S)</u>.

## LANGUAGE FOCUS ANSWERS

## PART C

1. Identify the noun that the pronoun "they" refers to in the second sentence of paragraph F.

   *the cities*

2. List the superlative adjectives found in the paragraphs M–R (e.g., "fastest," "slowest," "smallest," etc.)

   *the least; the world's largest; The largest; the largest; the most important; the largest; the most notorious; wealthiest; the third-largest*

3. In paragraphs M–P, identify present participles used in reduced relative clauses.

    i) *residing in cities will exceed seven billion*
    ii) *covering 3,100 miles*
    iii) *including most of England*
    iv) *shaping almost every aspect of human life and societal development*
    v) *arising from clustering and agglomeration on a regional scale*

4. List examples in the text of Greek or Latin roots affixed to English adjectives or nouns to create a new concept (e.g., "*mega*-cities").

    *megalopolis; geo-strategic; alpha (++) city; global cities dyad; nascent … technologies; hypercities; hyper-urban*

5. What phrase could best replace "when countless masses of people rise up" in paragraph S?

    e.g., *"when the people revolt"; "in a revolution"*

**Sentence Transformation**

6. Having to obey someone who is narcissistic and mean-spirited is not something most of us relish.
    **orders**
    Having <u>to take orders from</u> someone who is narcissistic and mean-spirited is not something most of us relish.

7. To resolve all the bugs in this program, we're going to have to start over from the very beginning.
    **scratch**
    To resolve all the bugs in this program, we'll be forced <u>to start from scratch</u>.

8. Take my advice: apply for promotion now, otherwise you're going to be left empty-handed.
    **cold**
    Take my advice: apply for promotion now, otherwise you're going to <u>be left out in the cold</u>.

9. The amendments to the labor agreement were ultimately very detrimental to the work force.
    **turned**
    The amendments to the labor agreement <u>turned out to be</u> very detrimental to the work force.

10. I'd strongly advise you to consider their proposal very carefully before giving your written consent.
**dotted**
I'd strongly advise you to consider proposal very carefully <u>before signing on the dotted</u> line.

# ULTIMATE CHALLENGE ANSWERS

## PART D

### Sentence Reconstruction

1. The Industrial Age in Europe brought with it the first recorded mass urbanization.

2. Rapid economic development in China has led to exponential growth rates of many urban centers.

3. Shifts in the balance of power toward the western Pacific have dramatically increased the importance of many cities in Asia and Australia.

4. Predictions are that by the middle of this century, a full seventy percent of earth's population will be living in urban centers.

5. Mass concentrations of humans in megacities place enormous demands on both the infrastructure and the environment.

6. Eco-cities are being designed to be largely self-sustaining through the use of renewable energy sources and water recycling systems.

7. Stark disparities in income between the rich and the poor have led to increased ghettoization in many urban centers of the developing world.

8. One major problem confronting urban planners and government officials in many areas of the developing world is how to provide the necessities of life for society's impoverished.

9. The primary goal of urban planners today is to create cities that function in greater harmony with our natural environment.

10. Environmentally friendly materials and technologies are helping developers to construct sustainable communities that do not damage sensitive ecosystems.

# ENGINEERING MARVELS

UNIT 9

CLOZE TASK ANSWERS

CLOZE TASK / READING PASSAGE: Suggested answers [responses may vary].

[1] what
[2] once / previously
[3] lower / reduce
[4] constructed / built
[5] producing / generating
[6] temperatures
[7] purpose
[8] physicists / scientists / researchers
[9] announced
[10] found / detected
[11] likelihood / probability
[12] certainty
[13] through
[14] involving / with / of
[15] extensive
[16] industry
[17] constructed / built
[18] patterns
[19] keeping
[20] ranging
[21] Relying
[22] terms
[23] associated
[24] width
[25] electricity
[26] equipped
[27] heights
[28] pipes
[29] withstand
[30] limit
[31] site / location
[32] near / along
[33] considered
[34] motion / movement

[35] cost
[36] view
[37] feature
[38] own
[39] time
[40] planet
[41] relation
[42] characterized
[43] role
[44] weight
[45] forth
[46] what
[47] words
[48] other
[49] conducted
[50] structural

## VOCABULARY WORK ANSWERS

### PART A

From Paragraphs A–K:      Synonymous Word or Phrase

1. theorized; postulated — HYPOTHESIZED (C)
2. enveloped; ringed by; circumvallated — ENCLOSED IN (B)
3. together with; joined with — COUPLED WITH (A)
4. sent around; spread around — CIRCULATED (B)
5. watched; viewed — TUNED IN (D)
6. existing in a concrete, material form — BRICK-AND-MORTAR (H)
7. gaps; empty spaces — VOIDS (H)
8. appear; manifest itself; present itself — TURN UP (E)
9. in succession; in series — IN A ROW (E)
10. sudden significant advances in science, technology, medicine, etc. — BREAKTHROUGHS (H)
11. residents; inhabitants — OCCUPANTS (H)
12. a type of rotor machine with blades or vanes that is driven by an air or water current — TURBINE (J)
13. integrate; include; encompass — INCORPORATE (I)
14. a process of removing salt from seawater — DESALINATION (I)
15. gigantic — MAMMOTH (J)

UNIT NINE | ENGINEERING MARVELS

| From Paragraphs L–V: | Synonymous Word or Phrase |
|---|---|
| 16. breaking; surpassing | SHATTERING (M) |
| 17. meeting point; intersection | JUNCTURE (O) |
| 18. made smaller; reduced in height or size | DOWNSIZED (N) |
| 19. gradually narrowed; slimmed | TAPERED (N) |
| 20. searing hot | SCORCHING (M) |
| 21. structures; external forms; figures | CONFIGURATIONS (O) |
| 22. climb; scale; move upward | ASCEND (P) |
| 23. rickety; delicate | FLIMSY (Q) |
| 24. tremors; earthquakes | TEMBLORS (Q) |
| 25. (figuratively): violence; ferocity; brute force | FURY (Q) |
| 26. hanging down; swinging | DANGLING (S) |
| 27. soundness; intactness | INTEGRITY (U) |
| 28. to slide back and forth sideways like a snake | SLITHER (T) |
| 29. happening at different times | ASYNCHRONOUSLY (T) |
| 30. belonging to the dominant, standard or principally accepted version of something | MAINSTREAM (V) |
| 31. dissipates; spreads out; scatters | DISPERSES (T) |

## PART B

VOCABULARY WORK ANSWERS

1. It seems natural in sprawling metropolises such as Los Angeles that many residents would prefer to shop online as opposed to spending an hour driving to a traditional <u>BRICK-AND-MORTAR</u> store, only to discover that the item is out of stock and would need to be ordered.

2. The discovery of the quantum mechanical nature of matter's most fundamental particles constituted a truly momentous <u>BREAKTHROUGH</u> in the human quest to understand the world we live in.

3. The odds of winning a major jackpot in the lottery are infinitesimally small, but one person's winning three times <u>IN A ROW</u> is simply phenomenal.

4. The long-term plan of leading visionaries is to INTEGRATE all of the Middle East and Northern Africa into a political-economic union with Europe.

5. Moral INTEGRITY consists of far more than merely following the letter of the law; it also entails treating others as you would want them to treat you, and viewing all others as ends unto themselves rather than as instruments for personal gain.

6. For children in many northern European societies, the passage out of childhood has traditionally been deemed a critical juncture in life when young adults assume the responsibilities of earning their own living and FENDING for themselves.

7. The genetic material of a virus is normally completely ENCLOSED within an outer protein coating, and in some strains also an external envelope.

8. Corporate DOWNSIZING has become a euphemistic synonym for laying off large numbers of employees.

9. Freud HYPOTHESIZED that the human psyche consisted of three functional domains, which he designated the id, the ego, and the superego.

10. The film star wore a flattering azure evening gown that was nicely complemented by a slew of sparkling sapphires DANGLING from her ears.

11. Hard copies of academic job applications should never contain letters of reference ENCLOSED within the same envelope. Today, the widespread use of email attachments has made hard copies and "snail mail" practically obsolete anyhow.

12. In many countries around the world, illegal OCCUPANTS of buildings are often forcibly evicted by the police.

13. In a great many disciplines, academic researchers experience quite early in their careers the tacit pressure to conform to MAINSTREAM thought; mavericks with unorthodox views are often weeded out early in the job selection process.

14. Evidence of malicious code or computer malware does not always TURN UP the first time the infected program is launched.

15. Albert Einstein recognized the special place that Johann Sebastian Bach OCCUPIES / OCCUPIED in the history of music when the physicist remarked that when God created the universe, Bach wrote the musical score.

UNIT NINE | ENGINEERING MARVELS

16. Patterns of economic development in northern and in southern Europe have been marked by a fairly high degree of ASYNCHRONY, with much of northern Europe characterized by a rational-bureaucratic state apparatus and advanced levels of industrialization, while southern Europe has been reliant on a decentralized collectivist framework typical of agricultural societies.

## PART C

1. Identify the noun clauses and their functions in paragraphs C and D.

   i) *that at even lower energies it might be possible to obtain evidence of the ....* [noun clause functions as the object of the verb "posited"]

   ii) *how and why particles have mass at all.* [functions as the object of the verb "explain"]

   iii) *that they has amassed (no pun intended) an overwhelming amount of evidence ...* [functions as the object of the verb "announced"]

   iv) *that the particle is 133 times heavier than a proton.* [functions as the object of the verb "mean"]

2. What does the word "This" refer to at the beginning of the second sentence in paragraph F?

   *CERN's use of the multinational collaboration network known as the "Worldwide LHC Computing Grid."*

3. Identify the main sentence subject and the main sentence verb in the second sentence in paragraph I.

   Main sentence subject: *plans*; main sentence verb: *incorporate*

4. Identify the verb tense and voice used predominately in paragraph H. In which other parts of the text is this tense/voice used? Why?

   *present tense, passive voice*. This tense and voice are used in most sections of the text that describe a research or construction process in which the agent or active subject ("doer") of the action is less important than the process or result.

5. How do you say the term "$m^3$"? How do you say the term "$m^2$"?

   $m^3$ = *cubic meters*; $m^2$ = *square meters*

LANGUAGE FOCUS ANSWERS

**Sentence Transformation**

6. After a year's worth of declining sales, the company is now near collapse.
   **verge**
   The company is now on the verge of collapse after a year's worth of declining sales.

7. The final 2,000 m of the climbers' descent was especially uncertain and dangerous.
   **touch**
   It was touch and go during the final 2,000 m of the climbers' descent.

8. Judith finally persuaded her husband to fly to the Bahamas on vacation instead of to Norway.
   **talked**
   Judith finally talked her husband into flying to the Bahamas on vacation instead of to Norway.

9. Margaret was very disappointed that none of her teammates would defend her during the negotiation process.
   **stand**
   Margaret was very disappointed that none of her teammates would stand up for her during the negotiation process.

10. I didn't really understand the hurtfulness of his comments until I got home.
    **sink**
    Not until I got home did the hurtfulness of his comments sink in.

## ULTIMATE CHALLENGE ANSWERS

## PART D

### Sentence Reconstruction

1. CERN's LHC is the most complex machine ever created by human hands.

2. The LHC was designed to create conditions similar to those that existed just moments after the universe came into being.

3. A sigma-five level of certainty implies that some causative principle other than chance is at work to effect a given phenomenon.

4 Many architects are using recycled materials such as car tires in the

construction of residential buildings.

5. Working under the assumption that the sky is the limit, architects continue to design taller and taller skyscrapers of dizzying heights.

6. Japan's pagodas are an engineering marvel because of their innate ability to withstand strong earthquakes.

7. The individual storeys in pagodas are not physically connected to one another but rather are simply placed on top of each other.

8. The staggered floors in the pagoda design permit the building to disperse the energy resulting from the lateral shifts that occur during an earthquake.

9. Architects and engineers rely heavily on high-speed computers and sophisticated programs to design structures that test the limits of civil engineering.

10. Many of today's engineering marvels are made possible through remarkable advances in materials science.

# UNIT 10

# GOING TO EXTREMES

## CLOZE TASK ANSWERS

CLOZE TASK / READING PASSAGE: Suggested answers [responses may vary].

[1] participant(s)
[2] endurance
[3] crumbling
[4] climbers
[5] spectacular
[6] entangled
[7] excitement
[8] deployment
[9] fatalities
[10] enticingly
[11] mistakenly
[12] realization
[13] breathe
[14] reliable
[15] visibility

[16] overpowered
[17] survival
[18] considerable
[19] horizontally
[20] patiently
[21] recirculate
[22] pleasurable
[23] infamous / famous
[24] photogenic / photographic
[25] height
[26] disoriented
[27] receptors
[28] chemistry
[29] endanger
[30] safety

UNIT TEN | GOING TO EXTREMES

# VOCABULARY WORK ANSWERS

## PART A

From Paragraphs A–J:　　　　　　　　Synonymous Word or Phrase

1. to climb — SCALE (C)
2. a dropoff; precipice — LEDGE (C)
3. entail; include — INVOLVE (E)
4. delicately; artistically — DAINTILY (C)
5. fearless, intrepid adventurers — DAREDEVILS (A)
6. in the grave; dead — SIX FEET UNDER (B)
7. ventures; adventures; undertakings — ENDEAVORS (B)
8. iffy; uncertain; unsure; shaky; unsecured — PRECARIOUS (C)
9. reserve; extra supply; replacement — BACKUP (E)
10. dangerous; perilous — TREACHEROUS (D)
11. protrusion; overhang — OUTCROPPING (D)
12. cliff; bluff — PRECIPICE (C)
13. merriment; glee; alacrity; elan — EXHILARATION (E)
14. plunge; nosedive — PLUMMET (C)
15. unswerving; unyielding; inexorable — RELENTLESS (E)
16. before; in advance of — PRIOR TO (F)
17. elevation — ALTITUDE (F)
18. mesh; interlacement; tight latticework — WEBBING (E)
19. resistance; the pull exerted on a wing to reduce downward motion — DRAG (E)
20. mazes — LABYRINTHS (H)
21. caves; grottos — CAVERNS (I)
22. jumping — LEAPING (G)
23. exploring caves — SPELUNKING (H)
24. having a strong fear of closed, tight spaces — CLAUSTROPHOBIC (I)
25. (noun) dives; drops — DESCENTS (J)
26. lethal; deadly — FATAL (J)
27. climb; upward movement — ASCENT (J)
28. rapid dive into the depths — PLUNGE(S) (J)

| From Paragraphs K–S: | Synonymous Word or Phrase |
|---|---|
| 29. anchored; fastened | SECURED (K) |
| 30. related to memory; helping the memory | MNEMONIC (K) |
| 31. of principal or prime importance | CARDINAL (K) |
| 32. far away; isolated | REMOTE (O) |
| 33. handling; manipulating; navigating | MANEUVERING (M) |
| 34. died as a result of; capitulated to | SUCCUMBED TO (P) |
| 35. changed | ALTERED (Q) |
| 36. split; cleft | CHASM (Q) |
| 37. inclination; tendency; proneness | PROPENSITY (R) |
| 38. courses of medical treatment or therapy | REGIMENS (R) |
| 39. deaths | FATALITIES (P) |
| 40. commencing; undertaking; venturing into; setting out on | EMBARKING ON (S) |
| 41. to contribute to or give to reluctantly | TO COUGH UP (S) |

> VOCABULARY WORK ANSWERS

PART B

1. At many companies and research institutes, employees are required to <u>BACK UP</u> their work into the company's external or cloud storage.

2. The <u>CARDINAL</u> rule of many fast-paced ball sports is this: keep your eye on the ball!

3. Helicopters, which routinely move forward and backward as well as up and down in rapid succession, achieve greater <u>MANEUVERABILITY</u> over conventional airplanes, but they also place greater demands on the flying skills of those who pilot them.

4. During the earliest years of European immigration to America, most of those who <u>EMBARKED</u> on the long journey by sea realized it was a one-way trip.

5. Cars with mid-position placement of the engine and rear-wheel drive are generally much more <u>MANEUVERABLE</u> than are other types of vehicles, which explains why this is the standard for Formula 1 vehicles.

6. International space exploration has never <u>ENDEAVORED</u> to send humans on the long voyage to Mars, though various plans to do so have been on the drawing boards for some time.

7. Airplanes of a blended wing design achieve much greater LIFT with significantly less power required, resulting in enormous fuel savings and greater overall stability.

8. When the horizontal stabilizer breaks or is rendered inoperable on an airplane, the craft PLUMMETS straight to the ground in a nosedive position.

9. Minor clothing ALTERATIONS, such as hemming the legs of trousers or letting out / taking in a few centimeters in the waist, do not require expert-level tailoring skills.

10. Light from the REMOTEST objects in the visible universe requires more than 13 billion years to reach us.

11. Specialists in human resources have repeatedly said that most job applicants get rejected simply because the candidates have failed to thoroughly research the company or institute PRIOR TO submitting their application package.

12. Although most snakes have a PROPENSITY to shy away from humans, both the Black Mamba of sub-Saharan Africa and the feared Taipan of Australia have actually been known to chase humans.

13. Many people refuse to conduct banking transactions online out of SECURITY concerns.

14. For someone who is severely CLAUSTROPHOBIC, the thought of being locked inside a closet would almost be as bad as being buried alive.

15. Transcontinental flights usually cruise at an ALTITUDE of approximately 10,000 meters.

16. All professional tennis players carry several BACKUP racquets just in case a string breaks.

## PART C

1. What is the implied meaning of the phrase "nature's most relentless force" in paragraph E?

    *gravity*

2. What is the implied meaning of the phrase "six feet under" in paragraph B?

    *dead and buried in a grave that lies six feet underground*

3. In paragraphs A–C, identify two reduced relative clauses that have been

LANGUAGE
FOCUS
ANSWERS

placed pre-positional to the noun subjects they modify.

> *Not content to challenge fate by merely sitting at the edge of a cliff hundreds of meters above the ground* [modifies the subject that follows: "the daredevils of extreme sports"]
>
> *Testing the limits of both skill and endurance* [modifies the subject that follows: "free climbers"]

4. Identify two types of conditionals found in paragraph P.

> Zero Conditional:  "When a 15-meter wave crashes down on a surfer from above"
>
> First Conditional:  "… if she's lucky."
> "Even if there are no obstacles below"
> "If a second or third wave then hits in rapid succession"

5. What phrase could replace the term "fail-safe" in the first sentence of paragraph I ("Without a proper fail-safe guide line anchored to the exit …")? What (if any) sentence modifications would need to be made to the original sentence if your suggested substitute phrase were used?

> *totally reliable; foolproof* [no changes necessary with either of these synonymous choices]

**Sentence Transformation**

6. You're going to be signing away your freedom if you agree to the terms of this contract.

    **up**

    Agreeing to the terms of this contract will essentially mean <u>giving up</u> your freedom.

7. The house is worth much more, so don't accept less than 50% more of all the standing offers.

    **settle**

    The house is worth much more, so <u>don't settle for less</u> than 50% more of all the standing offers.

8. I'm not able to answer questions of this nature so let me connect you to someone who can.

    **put**

    I'm not able to answer questions of this nature so let me <u>put you through to</u> someone who can.

UNIT TEN | GOING TO EXTREMES

9. Charlotte and James gave their daughter the name of Scotland's first queen.
**after**
Charlotte and James <u>named their daughter after</u> Scotland's first queen.

10. It's awful that the children were making jokes about the new boy's old clothes.
**fun**
It's awful that the children were <u>making fun of</u> the new boy's old clothes.

PART D

Sentence Reconstruction

1. Free climbers challenge fate by scaling the sides of rocks or mountains without any customary climbing aids such as ropes or picks.

2. Wingsuit jumpers rely on a traditional parachute to stop their fall during the last phases of their descent.

3. The most dangerous extreme sport in terms of total fatalities is cave diving.

4. Cave diving is especially dangerous because divers can easily become lost in the complex maze of underwater tunnels.

5. Divers who become disoriented may panic, which in turn may lead to rapid breathing and faster depletion of their oxygen supply.

6. The most valuable piece of equipment for cave divers besides the breathing apparatus is a guide line securely fastened to a position near the entrance to the cave.

7. Divers who ascend to the surface too quickly risk dying from a buildup of nitrogen bubbles in the bloodstream.

8. Surfing large waves is particularly dangerous in coastal areas that feature sharp coral reefs.

9. Full maturity in critical areas of the brain is required for a balanced assessment of the dangers involved in extreme sports.

10. Community-funded search teams are often called in to rescue extreme sports enthusiasts who find themselves trapped in adverse conditions.

ULTIMATE CHALLENGE ANSWERS

# UNIT 11
# NATURE'S AWESOME POWER AND LINGERING SECRETS

## CLOZE TASK ANSWERS

CLOZE TASK / READING PASSAGE: Suggested answers [responses may vary].

[1] teach
[2] strike / occur / happen
[3] else
[4] takes / runs
[5] capable
[6] region / area
[7] giving
[8] monitor / watch
[9] cover / shelter
[10] recorded / reported / measured
[11] so
[12] uninhabitable
[13] moving / sliding
[14] public
[15] withstand / resist
[16] equipped / constructed
[17] dampen / diminish / lessen
[18] disaster
[19] comparison
[20] blocking
[21] occurring / happening / possible but less likely: somewhere
[22] number / figure
[23] blanket / cover
[24] moment
[25] with
[26] add
[27] case
[28] too
[29] for
[30] Whatever
[31] Another
[32] emit

UNIT ELEVEN | NATURE'S AWESOME POWER AND LINGERING SECRETS

[33] What
[34] whether / if
[35] expansion
[36] light
[37] trying
[38] known
[39] attraction / pull
[40] exerted

## PART A

**VOCABULARY WORK ANSWERS**

From Paragraphs A–J:  Synonymous Word or Phrase

1. although; in spite of the fact that; even if — ALBEIT (B)
2. ordinary; everyday — MUNDANE (B)
3. giveaway indication; clue; revealing tip-off — TELLTALE (D)
4. funnel — VORTEX (D)
5. verbatim; as stated; word-for-word; in the strict sense of the word — LITERALLY (B)
6. cut off; amputate — SEVER (B)
7. meeting together; coming together; joining; intersection — CONVERGENCE (C)
8. anti-clockwise — COUNTER-CLOCKWISE (C)
9. incapable of being felt, seen, heard, tasted, or smelled — IMPERCEPTIBLE (E)
10. indefinitely long periods of time; billions of years — EONS (E)
11. the line around which a rotating body turns — AXIS (F)
12. incapacitating; rendering inoperable — KNOCKING OUT (F)
13. incomprehensible — UNFATHOMABLE (I)
14. liberated; set free; let loose — UNLEASHED (I)
15. desolating; demolishing; razing; destroying — DEVASTATING (I)
16. fortification; strengthening; bolstering — REINFORCEMENT (H)

| | | |
|---|---|---|
| 17. | use; utilize | EMPLOY (H) |
| 18. | late; behind time; behind an expected date or time | OVERDUE (J) |
| 19. | to quote or reference | CITE (J) |
| 20. | the large saucer-shaped basin that results from the explosion of a volcano | CALDERA (J) |

From Paragraphs K–T: Synonymous Word or Phrase

| | | |
|---|---|---|
| 21. | puzzle; mystery | ENIGMA (L) |
| 22. | spectacular; magnificent; eliciting a feeling of wonder and astonishment | AWE-INSPIRING (L) |
| 23. | fleeting glances; peeks at something | GLIMPSES (L) |
| 24. | in a manner that cannot be explained | INEXPLICABLY (M) |
| 25. | whole; entire; unbroken; undamaged | INTACT (M) |
| 26. | persons or things in contention for a role or position of some kind | CANDIDATES (N) |
| 27. | creating a need, requirement, or demand | NECESSITATING (N) |
| 28. | speculation | CONJECTURE (P) |
| 29. | lacking; wanting; sans; depleted of | DEVOID OF (P) |
| 30. | without any idea or inkling | CLUELESS (Q) |
| 31. | to resolve differences; resolve; reunite; unite | RECONCILE (T) |
| 32. | neighborhood; nearby area | VICINITY (S) |
| 33. | unseat; squash; subvert | OVERTURN (T) |
| 34. | framework; texture; cloth; structure | FABRIC (T) |
| 35. | fibers; threads; strands; strings | FILAMENTS (S) |
| 36. | desirous; avid; devouring | INSATIABLE (T) |
| 37. | strange; weird; abnormal; odd | BIZARRE (T) |
| 38. | vexed by; troubled by; struck by | AFFLICTED WITH (T) |

UNIT ELEVEN | NATURE'S AWESOME POWER AND LINGERING SECRETS

VOCABULARY WORK ANSWERS

PART B

1. The F5 tornado that struck late in the afternoon left behind scenes of total <u>DEVASTATION</u> over a 120 km² stretch of land.

2. Mirrorless cameras <u>EMPLOY</u> different types of sensors from those found in digital, single-lens reflex models.

3. Surprisingly, a great many employed adults find it more difficult to cope with <u>MUNDANE</u> tasks, such as grocery shopping, cooking, and doing laundry, than to deal with professional responsibilities at work.

4. In nearly all seismically active regions of the world, concrete for use in construction needs to be <u>REINFORCED</u> with fiber and/or steel rebar to bolster tensile strength, which is notoriously weak in concrete alone.

5. Professor Goodwine was accused of plagiarism for neglecting to <u>CITE</u> key passages he had extracted from a reference source.

6. Solar storms periodically emit charges of electromagnetic radiation so intense that they are capable of <u>KNOCKING OUT</u> important telecommunications satellites.

7. In the age of instant messaging, texting, and blogging, <u>CANDIDATES</u> for any political office must be especially careful not to do or say anything that might quickly come back to haunt them at election time.

8. One fundamental hallmark of all academic scholarship is the proper <u>CITATION</u> of referenced studies and resources.

9. Pilots often experience severe turbulence at the <u>CONVERGENCE</u> zones of thermally unequal air masses.

10. Individuals with chronic physical or mental <u>AFFLICTIONS</u>, such as amyotrophic lateral sclerosis, multiple sclerosis, or Alzheimer's, frequently require long-term intensive care.

11. One consistently contentious issue dividing the left and the right in the United States centers on recurrent attempts by pro-life social conservatives to <u>OVERTURN</u> the Supreme Court decision legalizing early-term abortions.

12. Residents living in the VICINITY / VICINITIES of major ports complain frequently about the stench of diesel fumes coming from ships' engines.

13. A bluish discoloration of the lips and the smell of bitter almonds from the mouth are two TELLTALE signs of cyanide poisoning.

14. Economically motivated migrants usually leave native countries or regions in search of EMPLOYMENT opportunities elsewhere.

15. Owners of vicious dogs are warned not to UNLEASH the animals in public places such as parks or playgrounds.

16. Tiger sharks exhibit a seemingly INSATIABLE appetite for any blood-containing flesh.

LANGUAGE FOCUS ANSWERS

PART C

1. Find instances of present participles in paragraphs A–F that have been used to connect sentences in a tighter manner than would otherwise be achieved using unreduced relative clauses.

   i) *wiping entire communities off the map and killing tens or even hundreds of thousands.*

   ii) *often giving rise to counterclockwise rotation.*

   iii) *signaling air rotation and the formation of a potentially deadly vortex.*

   iv) *giving residents in the best-case scenario a few, often critical life-saving minutes to take shelter.*

   v) *subducting under the Eurasian Plate and pushing the entire island of Honshu eastward toward North America …*

   vi) *killing thousands, destroying virtually the entire infrastructure of the region, and knocking out critical facilities at the Fukushima nuclear power plant.*

2. What verb tenses dominate in this reading passage? Why are these tenses used here?

   *Simple present to describe "timeless" facts (of nature); simple past to describe actual historic events.*

3. Identify two instances of grammatical parallelism in paragraphs E and F.

i)   ... *the earth beneath our feet seems to be the safest, most reliable, and most predictable feature* ...

ii)  ... *involve either thrust faults, on which an oceanic plate ... or strike-slip faults ... along which two giant plate masses slide* ...

iii) ... *killing thousands, destroying virtually the entire infrastructure of the region, and knocking out critical facilities at the Fukushima nuclear power plant.*

iv)  ... *threatens to make vast swaths of land uninhabitable for decades to come and to destroy much of the marine life in that region of the Pacific.*

4. Describe the semantic distinction between *farther / farthest* in paragraph O and *further* in paragraph R.

   *"Far" / "farther" / "farthest" refer to actual physical distances that can be measured; "further" refers to a degree of intangible / non-empirical abstraction, as in the intensity of argument or discussion.*

**Sentence Transformation**

5. I'm sorry to say that I'm not at all attracted to camping.
   **appeal**
   I'm sorry to say that <u>camping doesn't appeal to me</u> at all.

6. The investigators are interpreting the man's statement as being an admission of guilt.
   **amounts**
   The investigators feel that the man's statement <u>amounts to a</u> confession.

7. The company is risking everything to get this new product developed.
   **broke**
   The company is <u>going for broke</u> to get this new product developed.

8. The government is using lots of marketing tools and millions of pounds in resources to promote this national assistance program.
   **ground**
   To get this national assistance program <u>off the ground</u>, the government is using lots of marketing tools and millions of pounds in resources.

9. I'm sorry, but as much as I want to believe you, your explanation just doesn't add up.
   **sense**
   What you're saying just <u>doesn't make sense</u>, as much as I want to believe you.

**ULTIMATE CHALLENGE ANSWERS**

10. These tickets are freely available to the first 20 people who fill out a request form.
    **grabs**
    These tickets are <u>up for grabs for</u> the first 20 people who fill out a request form.

## PART D

### Sentence Reconstruction

1. Tornadoes, whose wind forces are measured on the Enhanced Fujita scale, are the most violent storms.

2. Tornadoes of the highest category are capable of nearly total devastation.

3. Tornadoes normally form at the convergence zones of highly dissimilar isothermal air masses.

4. Earthquakes occur when tectonic plates deep beneath the surface of the earth suddenly shift.

5. The largest earthquakes are generated along thrust fault zones in which one land mass is moving over or beneath another.

6. Strike-slip fault zones feature two land masses sliding past each other horizontally.

7. The magnitude of earthquakes is measured on the logarithmic Richter scale according to which the shaking amplitude of a temblor is ten times greater with every whole number increase.

8. Tsunamis are giant waves of water that form through the sudden shifting of land masses along the ocean floor.

9. Although infrequent in occurrence, eruptions of super-volcanoes are potentially cataclysmic events that can wipe out an abundance of life forms.

10. Physicists are perplexed by the fact that approximately ninety-five percent of all that constitutes our universe remains completely unknown.

# OUR BRAVE NEW WORLD

UNIT 12

CLOZE TASK / READING PASSAGE: Suggested answers [responses may vary].

[1] lineage
[2] analytical
[3] impressively
[4] extinction
[5] insufferable
[6] religious
[7] abstractions
[8] exclusive
[9] relationship
[10] inventive
[11] envisioned
[12] descriptive
[13] underlying
[14] prophecy
[15] causal / causative
[16] contestants
[17] programmers
[18] comparable
[19] accessible
[20] mimic
[21] justifiably
[22] Futurologists
[23] novelty
[24] molecular
[25] callousness

CLOZE TASK ANSWERS

# VOCABULARY WORK ANSWERS

## PART A

| From Paragraphs A–F: | Synonymous Word or Phrase |
|---|---|
| 1. sure signs; telltale signs or traits | HALLMARKS (B) |
| 2. of a hereditary lineage | ANCESTRAL (A) |
| 3. arcs or paths of flight | TRAJECTORIES (A) |
| 4. related to the concept of wholeness and to the idea that the whole is greater than the sum of its parts | HOLISTIC (C) |
| 5. related to understanding and knowing | COGNITIVE (C) |
| 6. related to the usefulness of something | UTILITARIAN (C) |
| 7. maintained the same rate of development; maintained the same speed | KEPT PACE WITH (C) |
| 8. forms or examples serving as models | PARADIGMS (B) |
| 9. intrusion; infiltration; invasion | INCURSION (B) |
| 10. a wrong name or title | MISNOMER (E) |
| 11. to produce in an automated manner | CHURN OUT (D) |
| 12. replacement; ersatz | SURROGATE (D) |
| 13. wonders | MARVELS (E) |
| 14. praised; extolled; hailed; commended | LAUDED (F) |
| 15. svelte; aerodynamic | SLEEK (D) |
| 16. appearing; emerging; coming into view; impending; threatening | LOOMING (D) |
| 17. related to an immediate period of time | SHORT-TERM (B) |
| 18. a point signaling the beginning of a change | CUSP (B) |
| 19. all-out; untempered; unabated; undiminished | UNMITIGATED (B) |
| 20. chemicals used to kill insects or other pests | PESTICIDES (B) |
| 21. deadly | LETHAL (A) |

UNIT TWELVE | OUR BRAVE NEW WORLD

22. destroying; reducing to nothingness — ANNIHILATING (A)

23. causing cancer — CARCINOGENIC (B)

24. area; forum; scene or place of an event, contest, or battle — ARENA (F)

From Paragraphs G–L:     Synonymous Word or Phrase

25. the will; the act of willing — VOLITION (H)

26. decoded; solved; unscrambled; figured out — UNRAVELED (H)

27. dazzlingly brilliant; glowing; shining — STELLAR (G)

28. ingenious; extraordinary; special; unprecedented — SEMINAL (J)

29. justification; grounds; reason; basis — WARRANT (J)

30. infinite knowledge — OMNISCIENCE (I)

31. occurring too soon or too early — UNTIMELY (K)

32. merciless; remorseless; compassionless — RUTHLESS (L)

33. future generations — POSTERITY (L)

## PART B

1. Grilled meats contain several dangerous <u>CARCINOGENS</u> that have been linked to stomach cancer and colon cancer.

2. Physicist David Bohm argued that mind and matter are integral aspects of a higher-order <u>HOLISTIC</u> universe whose essence is information.

3. Many neuroscientists argue that human <u>COGNITION</u> can be completely explained by a reduction of all thought processes to patterns of electrical activity in the brain.

4. Seating 150,000 spectators, Rungnado Stadium in Pyongyang, North Korea, is the largest sporting <u>ARENA</u> in the world.

5. The human capacity for mercy and compassion has not <u>KEPT PACE WITH</u> the development of our instrumental reasoning.

6. Cheating on exams produces at best <u>SHORT-TERM</u> gains at the

VOCABULARY WORK ANSWERS

expense of honest diligence and genuine understanding of the material being tested.

7. Until the dawn of general relativity and quantum mechanics in the early twentieth century, classical Newtonian physics had reigned supreme as the unquestioned PARADIGM of scientific inquiry.

8. The bite of the Common Krait (genus Bungarus), commonly found in southern Asia, is quite LETHAL, with a mortality rate of about 50% even for victims who receive antivenom.

9. The as yet only partially understood ability of cephalopods, such as the octopus and the cuttlefish, to camouflage themselves perfectly and almost instantaneously into the background patterns of their immediate environment is a truly astounding MARVEL of nature.

10. Married couples who for whatever reason are unable to conceive or bear children themselves often hire the services of a SURROGATE mother, who for pay becomes impregnated through in vitro fertilization.

11. Violinist Anne-Akiko Meyer's STELLER performance of the notoriously difficult Sibelius violin concerto was the true high point of the musical season.

12. UNRAVELING the mysterious origin of the Big Bang would likely be the greatest theoretical accomplishment in human history; the question is, however, whether the question itself is even answerable.

13. UNMITIGATED acts of cruelty and aggression are often telltale signs of severely impaired or undeveloped regions in the brains of individuals predisposed to sociopathic behavior.

14. The name "English horn" for the tenor member of the oboe family is a true MISNOMER because the double-reed woodwind is not English in origin, nor is it a horn.

15. Shy individuals often MARVEL at the ability of intrepid extroverts to strike up a conversation with virtually anyone, at any time, under any circumstances.

16. The ingestion of mercury primarily through the consumption of contaminated seafood often leads to significant COGNITIVE impairment and to kidney damage.

UNIT TWELVE | OUR BRAVE NEW WORLD

> LANGUAGE
> FOCUS
> ANSWERS

## PART C

1. Who is likely the intended audience of this text?

   *The general, moderately educated public.*

2. What type (genre) of text is this? What message is the author intending to send?

   *An expository essay.* {Answers may vary considerably.}

3. What two types of thought are being contrasted in this text?

   *The logical, analytical, spatio-temporal thought processes used in all types of calculations vs. the holistic, ethical, reflective, compassionate / merciful concern for life as such and for the planet in its entirety.*

4. In paragraph D, what does the possessive pronoun "their" refer to in the third sentence?

   *our computers / our surrogate selves*

5. What word could best replace "warrant" in the phrase "super-super-computer abilities to our most prized gadgets, often without warrant" in paragraph J?

   *justification; legitimacy*

### Sentence Transformation

6. Unfortunately, we had to close last year because too few people were using our services.
   **demand**
   Unfortunately, we had to close last year because there <u>was not enough demand for</u> our services.

7. We found the clerk's aggressive sales pitch very disconcerting and annoying.
   **aback**
   We were quite <u>taken aback by</u> the clerk's aggressive sales pitch.

8. We'd advise you to take full advantage of the low interest rates and shop around for better mortgage terms.
   **avail**
   We'd advise you <u>to avail yourself of</u> the low interest rates and shop around for better mortgage terms.

9. Would you like to contribute something for the birthday gift we're buying the director?
**chip**
Would you like <u>to chip in</u> for the gift we're buying the director for her birthday?

10. The Great Pyramids of Egypt have endured for millennia.
**test**
The Great Pyramids of Egypt have <u>stood the test of</u> time.

## ULTIMATE CHALLENGE ANSWERS

PART D

### Sentence Reconstruction

1. The human cognitive apparatus has permanently altered the conditions for life on planet earth.

2. Human interaction with the environment has resulted in the extinction of untold numbers of species.

3. The perfection of weapons capable of the total annihilation of all terrestrial life is a perversion of thought.

4. Instrumental reason's utilitarian conquest over nature has taken a heavy toll on the environment as a sustainable habitat for all forms of life.

5. Humans are much better at devising short-term solutions for problems than at comprehending the long-term synergistic effects of our activities.

6. Our preoccupation with consumer items is largely a result of the human tendency to abstract specific qualities from a given whole.

7. Machine learning involves the constant integration of positive and negative feedback into a computer system's database.

8. Computers like IBM's "WATSON" rely on enormous databases and elaborate probability algorithms developed by highly skilled programmers.

9. Some futurologists have predicted that computers will one day become self-aware, with the ability to self-replicate.

10. The human capacity for empathy has taken a back seat to our preoccupation with gadgetry and fads.

www.ingramcontent.com/pod-product-compliance
Lightning Source LLC
Chambersburg PA
CBHW082245300426
44110CB00036B/2448